"Elizabeth Crane has a way of looking at things, almost microscopically, that makes them appear strange and exquisite and infinitely dimensional and evanescent—like vanishing snowflakes. In *This Story Will Change*, she processes the sudden end of her long marriage by examining it through the prism of property, promises, dreams, expectations, and totemic objects, exploring the stories we tell ourselves and each other in the process of co-creating our lives. With characteristic humor, lightness, and grace, and much in the manner of a jeweler dismantling an intricate watch, Crane reveals marriage as a delicate machine for producing the illusion of permanence as bittersweet consolation against the constant, inevitable, irrevocable change that defines the human condition."

—Carina Chocano, author of *You Play the Girl*

"There is no writer like Elizabeth Crane. *This Story Will Change* gives us the first year of loss in all its confusion and upheaval; in this case, the gut punch of divorce. But Crane gives us so much more than a marriage memoir. It's how our bodies move forward—*one foot in front of the other, make it to the end of the day*—while our heads go back—*what the hell just happened and what could I have done differently?* The truth of it—in form and feeling as well as story—took my breath away."

—Megan Stielstra, author of *The Wrong Way to Save Your Life*

"Elizabeth Crane has written a luminous, devour-in-one-sitting, if-*Dept.-of-Speculation*-were-a-memoir, sly, hopeful, and intense deconstruction of her long marriage. If you ever had your heart broken, ever wondered whether memory plays tricks with you, or blamed someone else for things that might have been your own fault, read this book. I have been every person in this story in one way or another, and so have you."

—Gina Frangello, author of *Blow Your House Down*

This
Story
Will
Change

This Story Will Change

After the Happily Ever After

A MEMOIR

Elizabeth Crane

Counterpoint
Berkeley, California

This Story Will Change

Copyright © 2022 by Elizabeth Crane

First Counterpoint edition: 2022

Library of Congress Cataloging-in-Publication Data
Names: Crane, Elizabeth, 1961– author.
Title: This story will change : after the happily ever after / Elizabeth Crane.
Description: First Counterpoint edition. | Berkeley, CA : Counterpoint, 2022.
Identifiers: LCCN 2021052303 | ISBN 9781640094789 (hardcover) | ISBN 9781640094796 (ebook)
Classification: LCC PS3603.R38 T48 2022 | DDC 813/.6—dc23
LC record available at https://lccn.loc.gov/2021052303

Jacket design by Dana Li
Book design by Laura Berry

COUNTERPOINT
2560 Ninth Street, Suite 318
Berkeley, CA 94710
www.counterpointpress.com

Printed in the United States of America

1 3 5 7 9 10 8 6 4 2

For Janie and Michael

This
Story
Will
Change

Forever

Once upon a time in 2004 a woman and a man were married in a back-yard ceremony on a glorious September Saturday on the West Side of Chicago, handmade streamers in the trees, friends and family present to bear witness. They were happy and in love and people knew they were happy and in love. If anyone thought, Oh this is a terrible idea, they forever held their peace. Many of them spoke as the spirit moved them to share why they celebrated this love, and the celebration seemed genuine, and the couple was like, These people all get it, cool, we knew it, this marriage really is a good idea. But who knows, maybe someone did hold their peace. Maybe they could ask. They would have to ask everyone. They've lost touch with some of them. Sometimes on purpose. Which is not a thing you want to have to say about people who were at your wedding. What if someone held their peace and then they died? What if they got in touch with everyone who had been in attendance and every one of them said *No we didn't hold our peace, we were psyched for you*, but it was one or all of the people who died or lost touch who had held their peace? This wedding was fifteen years ago. Several people in attendance have died. Her dad died. The woman was so sure her dad loved her husband. But what if he was just happy that she was happy, and just crossed his fingers and hoped for the best? Or what if people lied about holding their peace, and said to their faces *We were not holding our peaces*, and/or what if everyone was just going along with this obviously doomed union, because let's face it, love isn't always enough, and maybe more than one person who died had extensive notes on why they thought this marriage was doomed, but held their peace, because they knew people did what they wanted, but then everyone died always having held their peace, leaving the couple to never know what they really thought and/or, moreover, maybe possibly in some universe, changing the course of the couple's history, you know, if they'd listened, and they were like *You're right, love isn't enough*, and they walked away and had lives that were better in ways they couldn't have imagined then, since everything seemed so great at the time, but instead they went ahead and got married, because they didn't know there were all these unspoken predictors of doom. If everyone held their peace, and then they died with all their peaces, how would the couple ever know? We were there. We doubt either of them would have listened.

Three Words

Just after New Year's, the married couple is in their bedroom, getting dressed for the day, and it's one of those moments when a person who's lived with another person for fifteen years knows something is on the other person's mind. The husband is oddly quiet, unresponsive, far away. Maybe the wife is being too cheerful this early in the morning. A million years ago she didn't like anyone talking to her in the morning either. Maybe it's annoying. Maybe it's one of those days. But she's gonna ask.

What's wrong?

Imagine a pause here that could be ten seconds but feels like ten hours. Granted, the husband is a long pauser. But this feels like the longest, tensest of pauses.

I'm not happy, he says. His eyes meet hers, finally. They're the eyes of a basset hound.

Now she's pausing, or maybe frozen entirely. Not breathing.

Three words. Three words that have probably been said millions of times by millions of people to millions of partners since words themselves existed, three words that a year later, having been replayed in my head countless times, never fail to leave me as breathless as I am in the moment he says them. The words that follow after the long pause don't help. I've more or less known he's been unhappy for a while. I've been calling it disconnected. Not present. We've talked about that. I know, of course, that in this moment, he's talking about the marriage. Okay. Thanks, I didn't know how to write that in third. Now we can get on to what he says next.

I have a crush on someone.

She knows immediately who it is, feels a little sick. It takes her a while to say anything.

Do you want to go to couples therapy?

He agrees to go to couples therapy, but let's be clear. His response is a damp *Sure*, or *Okay*, or maybe even *I guess*. It's probably *I guess*, because that feels the worst.

The wife claps her hands together. Her best friend calls this her signature move, the one she does when she's ready for some sort of action. They'll go to couples therapy. They'll work it out.

This Story Will Change

Listen. You're getting it as we're getting it. This story will change. That's really all we know for sure. This story is open to question, it's open to all the questions, this story is nothing but questions.

Easy

Once upon a time way before the husband came along, a woman was dating younger men. Not even remotely on purpose. There were just more of them who seemed to be available. It was fine. She could only go so much younger at this point, because she herself was young. Let's say it started when she was about twenty-seven or twenty-eight. There might still have been a scrunchie in her hair. She might still have been listening to Terence Trent D'Arby on her Walkman. And let's be clear: it was never inappropriate. In the early days of dating younger, it was never more than a few years. And one more thing: her fictional dream man has always been her exact same age, has her exact same pop culture references, like *James at 15*, or England Dan and John Ford Coley. There was one guy, when she was around thirty, who was way older, which was not an improvement, was a massive overcorrection age-wise, but this guy was wrong for her in ways that had little to do with how old he was. Then more younger guys after that, but again, only by a few years, that kind of age difference where twenty years later you realize you were always the same age. Sadly, as time went on, most of the men she met were somehow not getting older, they seemed to be getting five to ten years younger, and she did not see this as a plus; they were cute and interesting but generally had roommates and ate a lot of ramen (before the upscale ramen restaurant thing happened, just straight four-for-a-dollar ramen), and thought a great date was a Blockbuster video and ramen for two, with maybe some hot sauce added in to doctor it up, but she never liked spicy food, so only the guy's ramen was doctored up, hers was plain old undisguised ramen, twelve and a half cents' worth of ramen, served in mismatched cereal bowls, and this kind of dating went on for a couple years, nothing too serious, obviously, if the word *obviously* even needs to be added, and then in a more unfortunate turn, before this period of her life had passed, the term *cougar* came into popularity. And right about there she met the man who would become her husband, and she was forty-one and he was twenty-eight and the age difference was neither unnoticed nor unconsidered, but was ultimately put aside in favor of taking it one day at a time. Between them, at that time, they had one living parent. They knew loss. And they knew that they didn't know what was ahead in terms of who'd go first, because nobody gets to know that, and they were in love. They got along. It was easy. They got married. That was easy too. It was all easy, always.

Paper

They met in a church basement in Wicker Park that smelled like burnt coffee and the musty rummage-sale items that were always out for the taking, home to daily twelve-step meetings. Could be fine, but he was newly sober, she was not. On paper it looked pretty obviously not promising. There's a whole thing in their program literature about boy meeting girl on program campus having mixed results. Let's be real right now. Girl meeting boys, cute actors once upon a time, on a program campus, is one of the key things that kept this girl coming back when she was new. Not dating in your first year of sobriety is just a suggestion. She was thirty years old at that time. So, not a girl. She had already wasted too much time. She hadn't needed to drink over any of those cute actors, and they sure hadn't needed to drink over her either.

Thankfully by the time she met her future husband, she had enough good sense to think about someone else's sobriety, which brings us back to *on paper*. His presence in the room almost didn't register with her for a while, but then one time he shared something she related to, something about your bad thoughts always seeming more believable than the good ones, and they became friendly, in the way that people do who chat after a meeting and then walk the fuck away because one of them is depressed and still struggling to get sober and the other is ten years sober and feeling way less shitty about herself than she used to, less shitty enough not to choose a newly sober dude who's too young anyway. At this time she had a whole full life happening because she had taken the time to quit drinking and make better choices than she did when she was newly sober (go ahead and take it as a given that she made poor choices when she drank), and her first book was about to come out and didn't leave a lot of time for probably doomed crushes on too-young depressed newly sober boys. Who smoked. Then one day when future husband had maybe six or eight months of sobriety, he smiled for the first time, or it was the first time she saw him smile, and a great smile has always kind of been her thing, and so she was like, Oh, that depressed guy is actually really cute, but she put that aside because of him being new, didn't think much more about it, they talked after meetings once in a while, they talked at a sober picnic one time, later she went on a couple dates with a different younger guy, an even younger younger guy, here comes another, this guy was twenty-five and she was over forty; he'd written a sexy short story about her that made its way to her eyes, she got a mad crush because he was smoking hot in a way she ordinarily didn't much care about, like he'd stepped out of a Ralph Lauren ad in a fisherman sweater and thick blondish curls, with a gentle breeze and natural light and two yellow labs that found him wherever he stood, and so when you throw the sexy short story in on top of the sexy dude, forget about it. She was dunzo. Or dunzo for a week or ten days, before her future husband came along, which was around the same time. She had one date with sexy gentle breeze dude and then didn't hear from him and spent some time wondering why and she knew she was too old for that waiting-for-phone-calls shit but wasn't quite ready to hang it up either, meanwhile here comes future husband, with his depression and his new sobriety and his youth, and they started hanging out and then she had one more date with Breezy, and sitting across from his perfect face, in and out of whatever he was saying, all she could think was, I just want to be with that other guy. So that's what she did. She went to be with that other guy, even though they were still just friends, and she had no plans to make any sudden moves and wasn't sure if what they had could or should ever be romantic anyway, like we said, it didn't look good on paper. He was a smoker. That alone had always been on her list of deal breakers. Actually at the time it was the only thing on the deal-breaker list. Her mom had died of lung cancer. Smoking is gross. Depressed young newly sober smoking guy called her later when he said he'd call her later, stopped by her apartment after work every other day just to say hi; one of those times, he tried to rescue an unwell baby bird on her back porch, gave it some droplets of water, warmed it up in his hands, this was probably the tipping point for her, sensitive dude who rescues baby birds, and he had pretty hair too, actually, soft and shaggy, and his eyes sparkled when he smiled, and then finally after a couple weeks of hanging out he came to take her to dinner at that place that used to be a train station, and he was wearing a nice wool shirt, and holding a bouquet of purple flowers, and it's only then, a couple weeks into them hanging out, with the shirt and the flowers, that she realized he'd liked her the whole time. So one month shy of his one-year sober anniversary they officially started dating. *I saw you across the room when I was new and I thought to myself, She is a stone-cold fox and when I get a year I'm gonna ask her out,* he said. A year, eleven months, whatever, rules were made to be broken, she thought, especially when they're only suggestions and anyway, don't tell me what to do.

Fine Therapy

Finding a couples therapist where they live turns out to be not so easy. They have coverage for it, but their area is remote enough that without a referral, it's going to be trial and error. Not to mention that asking anyone in their very small city in the Hudson Valley for a referral seems likely to equate to announcing it in the paper. Also the husband doesn't want to participate much in finding one. He wants the wife to find several, and then for him to choose.

They meet two.

He prefers one for reasons the wife isn't clear on. This therapist has an office upstairs in a Victorian carriage house with a big old unrestored window, which seems like it might be a good enough reason for him. The wife would describe this therapist as seeming *fine*, which is maybe a low bar. But it's been a month of looking and the wife wants to get started. So every other week they go to couples counseling and the therapist asks what they each want and they tell her some things they want. Some of these things aren't out of the blue after fifteen years. The husband wants more affection, he wants excitement, he wants the wife to cook, and to go hiking, maybe bike riding in Central Park, he wants the wife to plan things for them to do, he wants more sex or he wants her to initiate sex or he wants sex later at night or he wants some other kind of sex that they aren't having or he wants all those sex things, but he does not want any of the sex things to be planned. He wants the wife to stay up later at night and to not fall asleep watching TV and to be a better navigator in the car and to overall *take care of him better. Differently.* The wife wants the husband to take her on a vacation, be kind, commit to working on himself more, outside of couples therapy, on his own, to look at himself as deeply as she believes he once did. The wife wants the husband to read her most recent book.

Everything Is Fine

They don't go bike riding. They don't go on vacation. They do some of those other things. He reads her book. He is more kind. She cooks, a little. She stays awake. She tries to be more affectionate, though because he is so affectionate already, sometimes she forgets that he wants a little more from her direction. They do some sex things.

Outside therapy, maybe the third time they go, they're parking the car and before he gets out, the husband sort of jokingly says *I don't want to do this. Why are we doing this? We don't need to do this. Everything is fine!*

The wife laughs, because she sure as shit doesn't want to do this either, but everything does not seem fine. She may not know what is wrong exactly, but maybe fine is not the base level you're looking for in a marriage. And so far, the therapist is not even helping them level up a notch above fine. Maybe that's the whole idea when the therapist themself is only fine. More than once, the wife has to translate between the therapist and the husband. The therapist's style is to slowly recalculate like a GPS when you keep turning the car around. She starts with an idea, she'll say *Okay, let me put it like this.* And she'll begin some kind of parallel, but not even get far enough for a germ of the idea to emerge, before she stops herself and says *No wait. Let me put it this way.* And she'll start to put it that way, and then she repeats this cycle several times until she finishes a complete thought. Occasionally the wife finds it a useful thought, just as often, not. Just as often, the husband doesn't get it at all, which is when the wife provides a pared-down version for the husband. *She thinks we need a vacation.* Next in the communication sequence is that the husband will start to say something, but her husband is a slow talker, takes long pauses between phrases in a complete sentence (more so when he really doesn't want to say something), and even though the wife can usually figure out where he's going, the fine therapist often doesn't fully follow, at which point the wife has to translate back for her. *He wants me to plan it,* the wife says to the therapist, and this two-sentence exchange takes place over the course of ten or fifteen expensive minutes of their not-covered hour because this therapist does not work with their insurance provider. They see this therapist every two weeks, six times over the next two months.

Inventories

A Post-it note from when they were first dating. *I love B_*, red pen, yellow Post-it. Curlicues all around. The most artful of Post-it doodles. He's an artist. She puts it in a frame, and it goes on her bookshelf. For always.

A crude wooden heart, with a scalloped edge, *I love you* carved into it.

Another wooden heart, pink stripes going out from a point at the center.

Another wooden heart, whittled, smooth, fits in her palm.

A heart made of plaster, pale pink. *I love you.*

A heart made of sand.

A heart cut from glass, etched with their initials.

A giant cardboard heart, painted pink, *I Luff You.*

She may have asked for some of them and doesn't care that she had to. She is dissuaded from bringing the cardboard one in a move. Later he suggested that for display purposes she curate.

She made things for him too:

A banner, hearts cut from vintage wallpaper.

A banner, hearts cut from a Sears Christmas insert from 1969.

An embroidery, *I love you so much you are the best hunny bunny for ever and ever.*

A cross-stitch that reads *wool or copper*, for their seventh anniversary.

A vintage ledger of *I love you*s, in collage, her wedding gift to him.

He did not ask for these either, but he loved them all the same. He said he did.

Prior to this, the totality of gifts from the totality of boyfriends from the inception of having boyfriends in 1979 to the end of having boyfriends in 2003:

A wobbly plastic penguin.

A pair of vegetable-shaped bobby pins.

A pair of socks with bows printed on them.

A small wooden planter with a packet of seeds.

An *Us* magazine and a *People* magazine.

A tiny cactus.

A copy of Billy Joel's *Cold Spring Harbor*, the original version, recorded at the wrong speed. That was a good one. He loved her. She was seventeen. She broke up with him shortly after that, of course.

So.

From the husband again:

A bookshelf. That he built. For her. The wood is fancy. It has a special shelf in the middle for the vintage typewriter that came out of her grandparents' barn.

A window seat in their Brooklyn apartment. That he built. For her. With trim to match, like it was there from when the building was built.

A powder room, made out of what had been the hall closet.

A hall closet, made out of a sliver of space at the top of the basement stairs.

Floors refinished. Walls sanded and plastered and smoothed.

Another bookshelf, this one built in, a hidden surprise behind the bedroom door.

A bathroom gutted and remodeled. Subway tile, a vintage claw-foot tub. She wishes you could see the patina. Layers of blues and greens.

A kitchen gutted, brand-new wood floor, custom-built cabinets, new appliances except for a vintage stove. Fully functioning, not completely finished.

Math

The husband tells the wife he wants to be seduced minus the wife is not a seductress plus the wife does her best to play the role for a minute minus the wife is not an actress or a seductress plus an off-campus seductress equals seduction.

What Marriage Is

Other than marrying her Barbie and Ken in third grade (repeatedly), the wife didn't think that much about marriage until someone she loved proposed that they do it. Or, she thought it might be nice, with the right person. But it wasn't until she met someone who seemed right, and then said yes, that she started thinking about what marriage actually was, or could be or should be for her. She became very curious about other people's marriages suddenly, not enough to get overly nosy, since she knew that the only way to really know someone's marriage was to be inside it. She only knew how she didn't want to do it, which was how her mom and stepdad did it, which involved a fair amount of yelling. She had no memory of how her mom and dad did it, only that they decided to undo it. And because being a kid of divorce was bad enough to want to avoid a situation where that undoing was a possible outcome, she waited, and she waited, and then she said yes.

I Will Make You Sandwiches

And so she was a wife. She had been single forever and she became a wife and she didn't cook because she never cooked and in these modern times you don't have to cook to be a wife. You can work. You can cook or not cook. You can be a modern wife. You can like baking, like our wife, and not like cooking. You can dislike baking and cooking both. But her husband asked if she'd try so she tried. She wanted to please the husband because he did so much to please her. She gave cooking a good go. She thought, My mom had a career, but she somehow did this, I could do this. Early in the marriage, she made dinner, simple dinners, pasta, fish, a vegetable, a salad, rice. Once or twice she made his mom's chicken recipe. She might have given more consideration to how that might go. *It's good, but it's not my mom's.* Once or twice she made rice; her husband said *It's easy. Two cups water one cup rice. Boil the water, add the rice, turn the heat down, cover the pot, fluff.* Once or twice, she burned it. Once or twice, he stood over her, watching. Once or twice, she told him to make it himself or let her just burn it but please right now just go away. Why *did* my mom do this, she thought. *I will make you sandwiches for lunch,* she told the husband. *That's the best I can do.* She made a little chart of sandwiches he liked, which condiment and which cheese went with which bread and which meat, and she made him sandwiches to take for lunch, and she stopped making dinner.

I Will Bake You Cookies

Like we said, she did enjoy baking. Mostly cookies, but a cake now and then. She baked him a heart-shaped cake for Valentine's Day in their last year together. She found a recipe for snickerdoodles, and she tweaked it a bit (+ brown sugar) and tweaked it a bit again (+ an extra stick of butter) and those snickerdoodles were fucking good. She wore a vintage apron when she baked because the flour always went everywhere but it happened that he found her sexy in the apron and hugged her from behind when she wore it and at the end there were snickerdoodles and he really, really liked the snickerdoodles, but he still wanted a meal.

Dinner Though

In the last few months of their marriage they try two new things: one month they do the Whole30 (takeaway: going off sugar and dairy and everything that makes anything worth eating for thirty days will not save your marriage, you're welcome) and they subscribe to a meal-kit service and three nights a week she makes dinner. Let it be said: a meal-kit service is still legitimately cooking. It saves you the shopping. But it's a full cooking situation. The ingredients come in a box and they do not cook themselves. Most meals have three components. Meat, vegetable, starchy thing. Per the recipe card, total time involved ranges from thirty minutes to fifty minutes including prep. Not noted on the recipe card: stress level. You get a hot-pepper symbol if it's spicy but you don't get a brain-explosion emoji if it's extra stressful. So she breaks it down. She washes and preps the vegetables and puts them in bowls like you see on cooking shows or gets them ready on a pan to go into the oven. She puts together any of the sauces that she can have ready, another bowl. She preps the meat, puts that on a plate ready to go in the pan later. She goes back to her work. The husband gives her a heads-up about when he'll be home, and she does the actual cooking accordingly. But even with instructions, the reality is that getting these things to all come out finished and hot at the exact same time is not an equation that can be calculated, and god bless you if you have the innate ability to do this, but this is the part that for her makes the whole endeavor completely unpleasant.

Plus thirty to fifty minutes is usually more like forty-five to seventy. This should be in the advertisements, frankly, at least in the fine print. *For some of you, double the time.* How does anyone find time to do this? How do people with children do this? This is the element that surprises her. She would rather go to the gym with this supposed extra time, and she doesn't want to do that either. In theory she thought she had the time. Anyone could spend that much less time on the internet, couldn't they? Her husband for sure thinks she has the time. In the afternoons, a lot of her work consists of reading, whether it's reading student work or reading as part of being a writer. It turns out that time taken plus stress incurred of trying to get the three components hot at the same time plus pressure of wanting to please the husband equals a level of mental exhaustion that cuts into her work time above and beyond the thirty to seventy minutes. One time, as often happens, she doesn't get the timing quite right, and she burns the mushrooms and onions just as the husband walks in, and she drops the hot pan, creating a small but permanent mark on the floor, the wood floor that her husband has laid in and finished himself. The wife, near tears, says *I really don't like cooking*, and the husband is pissed about the floor, doesn't say that in so many words, but his entire body reads *I should tell her it's okay, but I don't want to. She messed up my floor.*

Most of the meal-kit meals end up being pretty good, and the husband expresses gratitude to the wife for the effort, as well as for sitting down to dinner together with the wife, which they mostly only do if they go out or order in, which they do often enough but not every night. She has been happy to eat salad every night, hours before he gets home from work. She doesn't like to eat right before bed, and he tends to be home from work later than she wants to eat and we don't need to get too deep into how digestion works here but she likes to start winding down fairly early in the evening, maybe by eight, which is occasionally when these dinners are finished, at which time she likes to hang out in bed and he likes to sit on the sofa because he hasn't been sitting there for most of the day, as she has, and why wouldn't he want to enjoy all the rooms of his house.

I Will Never Leave You

A couple years into the marriage, the husband and wife decided it was time to get a dog. The wife was teaching a few college classes but mostly working at home, and it seemed like a nice thing for a dog, to have someone mostly at home. The dog they chose was a sickly, skinny, low-key Catahoula rescue when they first brought him home, but soon enough he was a healthy eighty-pound puppy, which was a bit of a surprise, since they'd been told he was close to a year old when he was found and therefore surely full grown, only to see him more or less double in size, all this to say that training him became a bit of a challenge for the wife. They took him to an eight-week training class and he learned to sit and to stay and to drop it, to take it and to leave it, and he got his photo taken at the end of eight weeks with a photocopied diploma and a mortarboard on his head. *Come*, this was never the dog's favorite, and *Heel*, well, that really never took. She blamed herself for this and the husband basically blamed her too. *We have to be consistent,* he said.

I know, she said. *It's hard.* He indicated frustration. She cried.

He said *I love you. I'm not leaving.* He had been aware of her abandonment issues, and taken it upon himself to provide ongoing reassurance that abandonment would not occur. He would go on to say this many more times in their future. He would say this every time they had conflict. They did not have that much conflict, but he would say this every time. She hoped she would believe him one day. They would stay married for many more years, and as those years went on, it seemed more and more believable that they might stay married forever.

At forty-one, she brought nothing but furniture, books, abandonment issues, and theories to the relationship; she'd always had theories, which is to say that her relationship history prior to the husband is arguably nonexistent. There had been a few three-to-six-month deals, one that lasted a year and a half, with four breakups. She had a low threshold for fighting or abusive behavior, no threshold at all for being called a cunt, a higher threshold for boring conversation, if the dude was sexy enough, a higher one still for dubious behavior that's harder to pinpoint, and a way higher one for unavailability. Back in the day, this was really her thing; she could always get behind a guy she couldn't have. She liked her story that she usually knew how it was going to go with a guy from the beginning, that if she made a poor choice, she knew what she was doing. She would take the responsibility and the ride. Maybe it would be fun. You never know. Dating a comic you meet on the Atlantic City boardwalk might turn out just fine. Her main theory about a real and long-term relationship was that it shouldn't be that hard. Show up, compromise, say what you mean to the best of your ability. Something like that. She brought this theory into her marriage and it turned out to be true. She was pleased. The hardest part, always, was believing he wouldn't leave. Any and every conflict they had, no matter how small or how mercifully infrequent, her mind would go to him leaving. Thoughtful in a conflict, he always offered preemptive reassurance. *I'm not leaving,* he'd say. *This isn't a big deal,* he'd say. *I promise. I love you. I will never leave you.*

They finally got one of those harnesses that the dog couldn't pull on, which helped.

She began to turn a corner somewhere around their tenth anniversary. Wow, she thought, he hasn't left. Ten years is a long time. He still really loves me. I guess he's not leaving.

Fix This

A couple weeks after they begin a trial separation and the husband moves out, a neighbor she doesn't know comes banging on her fence and screaming at her because his dog has gotten loose and she has gotten freaked out because her dog, on leash, often doesn't do well with loose dogs. She can control her dog but is not prepared to break up a dogfight between two eighty-pound dogs. Thankfully she doesn't have to on this occasion, but this neighbor accuses her of being unfriendly, of having once called the cops on him about trash on his property. She has not called the cops on him or anyone else. Her husband has once called this neighbor's landlord about the trash around their building, having nothing to do with this neighbor, which may be the source of his confusion. She remains calm while she is being yelled at, tries to be reasonable, but he just wants to yell. This is the kind of thing that usually makes her want to move, but she's out of moves. It is now the kind of thing that makes her pick up the phone and call her husband screaming. *Just come back. Just get your shit together and come back and fix this. I can't do this by myself. I can't. I can't do it. I can't do it. I can't do it.*

Needs

I need you to know that I loved him. I need you to know why I loved him. I need you to know all of the reasons I loved him. I need me to know why I loved him. I need you to know that I stayed for fifteen years for a reason. I need to know that there is a reason. I need to know what the reason is. I need to show you all the beautiful moments. I don't want to bore you with happy tales, I don't want to create unhappy tales, I don't want to only tell sad tales. I don't want to make him into a bad guy. I don't want to be the bad guy. I don't want there to be any bad guy. I need to do the math of my marriage and I need for it to add up to something that makes sense. Perhaps I need a ledger. I need for the good column to be longer than the bad, I need to see the marriage totals in front of me, I need for there to be accounting. I need to believe the people who tell me I didn't waste fifteen years, that endings and failures aren't the same thing.

They Were Thankful

He always thanked her for doing the dishes, or picking up a prescription, or cleaning the bathroom, whatever like this, and she always thanked him for taking out the trash, or vacuuming, or paying the bills or whatever like this. They thanked each other all the time for these ordinary things. They thanked each other for loving each other. All the time.

They Said Nice Things

He told her he loved her every day until the end. She told him she loved
him every day until the end. He said nice things all the time. All the
time. She said nice things all the time. They said fifteen years of nice
things. They said no mean things ever, they said only nice things. *You're
the best wife. You're the best husband. We're the best couple. We win marriage. You're the most sexy and the most awesome and the most talented
and the most smart and you have the best style and you're so good to me
and I'm so lucky and so grateful that you are my wife and I will always,
always, always love you.*

New Dream

He had always dreamed of getting married, having kids, owning a home, fixing up a home. She hadn't not dreamed of these things. She'd been working on other dreams. She had dreamed of not moving any more times. She dreamed of Chicago, and she moved to Chicago. She did not dream of leaving.

When they were still dating, they went for a walk around his neighborhood in Pilsen; he showed her a house he had once wanted to buy. They married, they talked about kids, they looked at houses, there was one he was sure he wanted to buy; the wife was less sure about that particular house, that particular house smelled like pee, needed more work above and beyond pee remediation than she felt prepared to endure; they began the loan application process, decided together that it was not a good idea to buy this particular house. They tried to have kids (briefly, so briefly), that didn't happen, the wife was not moved to put her body through what might be necessary to make that happen, they looked into adoption, the husband decided he wanted to go to art school, they decided together to table everything related to kid making. They moved to Texas, he went to art school, decided children were the worst, *So glad we never did that,* he said, he graduated from art school, they moved to New York City so the husband could be an artist. They moved to New York from Texas knowing they might not stay forever, so she said *I have one more move in me.* He indicated that he understood.

They found an apartment in Brooklyn that they loved but which was too small and too expensive to be forever, they lived there amid boxes they never unpacked because where would that stuff even go, they heard about a small historic city upstate, a short train ride from the city. They visited the historic city, were charmed by the historic city, views of the Hudson, historic architecture, they went back to the historic city, they looked at historic houses, they picked a historic house, they went through the loan application process and all the other home-buying processes and they bought the house and they closed on the house and they got the keys to the house and they took that excited *We're homeowners now!* photo that you're required to take by the front door on the day you get the keys to the house.

The husband gutted and rehabbed the bathroom to her liking with a claw-foot tub and penny tile on the floor. It was no trouble for the wife to frequently tell the husband how happy and grateful she was to him for making her this super sweet, shiny new bathroom. She was so continually delighted by it that it would have been trouble for her not to. The husband also gutted and rehabbed the kitchen to her liking, with subway tile and a farm sink (with a disposal!) and a fridge (with an icemaker!) and a dishwasher and cabinets he built himself, ones that hide the trash and the recycling and the dog food bin, and he refinished the floors upstairs (there's an upstairs!), for which she was also grateful, and he patched and painted the walls and the ceilings and he fixed things when they broke and she was grateful for all of it. They decorated together, but the decorating budget was limited, so it came together piecemeal. They hung art and put their books on shelves and they got their first new sofa and they got a new bed and they set up a guest room, that had been a dream of hers, to have a guest room that was only a guest room, and not a guest room and an office, and they now had two separate rooms for these functions, a dream now realized. Plus a little backyard and a carriage house/barn, which was a fun thing to say, *Yeah, we have a carriage house!* or *It's in the barn!* Who lives in a city and gets to say they have a barn? The husband used the carriage house/barn for a woodshop and whatever else. Her grandparents had a barn filled with a hundred years of miracles.

A few years later the husband has a new dream, having let go of two parts of the original three-part dream. *Maybe we could co-own the house,* he says.

Not So Fine

Once upon a time a woman's husband leaves and she spends a few months in her house crying to friends on the phone all day and doesn't go anywhere besides maybe Target or the grocery store because she doesn't want to run into the husband at one of the two coffee shops or restaurants in the tiny downtown where everyone goes. She goes to Fire Island for a week to see her best friend, she goes to Vermont to see friends, she goes into the city once a week or so to see friends, these interludes help, but every time she goes back to her house she also goes back to crying to friends all day, as though he has just moved out the day before, even though a couple of months have somehow passed since the husband left. Then she goes to the city for a week to be with friends. A fancy pal and his wife offer her their fancy pied-à-terre in the East Village, and that's better, she wonders why she hasn't thought of going to the city sooner, she actually thought she was fine in her house, she loves her house, she feels comfortable in her house, it's her house, the house itself isn't any different now, the house did nothing wrong, yes, his stuff is still there, his art, his grandfather's secretary, the fifties modern TV cabinet he pulled off 14th Street and restored to its glory, his dad's old metronome next to her dad's old metronome, okay, maybe some redecorating will be in order, but still, it never feels to her like the stuff or the house itself is the problem, it doesn't even feel like being alone in the house is the problem, eventually it occurs to her that being alone anywhere now is a problem, but that she might be somewhat less alone in the big city than in the little city where her house is and where her husband and his girlfriend are.

Particularly annoying side thought is that there was a time when being alone had not been a real problem for her, at least insofar as she had always chosen to be alone over settling for someone so as not to be alone. She's an only kid raised primarily by a single parent who often traveled. She knows how to occupy her time. She was not a kid who got bored. She was a kid who read, a kid who wrote, a kid who put on original plays in the tiny hallway by the elevator in her apartment building, who became an adult who read and wrote books that got made into plays that went into actual theaters. She stayed single until she was forty-one because she didn't meet anyone she wanted to share her life or her space with until she met the man who became her husband. She remembers thinking, after having moved to Chicago and finally having the luxury of a broken-down but roomy two-bedroom apartment, Where would I ever put another person in here? She didn't know that she'd work that out easily when the right person came along. (A right person? What does right person even mean now?) They'd surely have to get two more rooms just for him, wouldn't they? The point of the annoying side thought is that she was mostly fine being mostly alone for much of her life before he came around, lonely sometimes, sure, but after fifteen years of living with another person, is no longer so fine with being mostly alone. She's fine alone knowing another person, thankfully one she loves, is going to be there at the end of the day, the end of the work trip. At the end of the marriage, not so fine alone. Not so fine.

This Story Will Not Be a Fairy Tale

It's not a fable, or a fairy tale, or a folk tale, or a tall tale. It's a straight-up true tale. Which will change.

The Time They Go to Woodstock

They drive up to Woodstock for a film festival. The wife has adapted her first novel into a film and it's showing at a festival in Woodstock that isn't too far from their house, so they hit the road and plug in the music and they pick an excellent mix of upbeat driving-to-see-your-own-movie pop songs curated from across the last several decades, Rose Royce and the Manhattans and Queen and even some NSYNC and some Bieber, and they sing along and dance in their seats and the wife makes them into Instagram stories because that's what she does, and they laugh and hold hands and sing all the way to Woodstock. They go out to dinner with the cast and crew in Woodstock, they watch the movie, everyone loves the movie, or they lie convincingly about it, anyway. For the drive home they put on a more low-key playlist from across the last several decades, Linda Ronstadt, Elton John, Carole King, and even Bradley Cooper singing "Maybe It's Time" from *A Star Is Born*, which is a bit of a sneak attack because she's just been saying she wasn't so sure about Bradley Cooper singing and since it makes her cry she's forced to concede that it's a very good song indeed, and it's definitely a case where she was a wee bit attached to some contempt she'd formed prior to investigation.

The first song on the way up, his pick, is CeeLo's "Fuck You." The wife laughs and laughs.

Because it isn't the husband and wife, it's the wife and one of her oldest and dearest friends and his teenage kid. They go back to her house upstate after the movie and they eat ice cream and they stay up late talking and laughing. At one a.m. the kid says she's tired and the wife and her old buddy tell her she can go to bed, and the kid, who seems way too cool to want to hang out with her dad and his friend for long, says she doesn't want to go to bed because she will have FOMO and the wife says *Me too*, and so they all stay up until three a.m.

This Guy

Her old buddy is a storyteller. Can quote things you said thirty years ago and describe the dress you were wearing when you said it. Drinks double iced espresso because he has *no time for coffee to cool, needs it in*. He's tall. He's handsome. Big blue eyes, full post-fifty head of thick wavy hair. He's an actor. He should have a one-man show. He is a one-man show. He should have a play. He should have so many plays. They've been friends for nearly thirty years, since they were babies, since her early sobriety. Know this for now: everything about him is big. Big fun, big personality, big heart, big ideas, big faith.

The Client

But let's look again at the last year of this marriage. The husband took on a new client who owned a large Victorian home with large Victorian windows she wanted to restore. The husband was not attracted to the new client. The client was the physical opposite of the wife. The client was the actual opposite of the wife. The wife wore jeans and boots and sneakers and t-shirts and vintage cardigans always, the client was about voluminous layers of fabric and sandals. The wife was not loud, but the client seemed quiet. No quickly discernible personality. Had a long, jagged nose that reached to her chin and ended with a giant mole, and wore a pointy black hat.

Boring

It's a boring story of happiness. Do you want to hear all their nicknames for each other? Do you want to hear all their running jokes? One time she told him she was bringing home a special treat, and he asked *Is it astronaut ice cream?* She still thinks that's cute and goofy and very him, but do you get it? Do you need to? Do you want to hear about the time they went to see Sonic Youth in that industrial park on the West Side and nothing bad happened between them, or the time they went to see Yo La Tengo at the Riviera and nothing bad happened between them? Or do you want to hear how they went to see Ben Folds at the Chicago Theatre and he thanked god they had seats, he was never going to a show where he had to stand ever again, because maybe, maybe this was the beginning of something, maybe it was nothing, but maybe it was a shift toward boring in a bad way versus boring in a good way. Maybe it's not boring at all, maybe it's just what happens when you're not twenty-eight anymore and you've worked all day and you want to see a concert but you also want to sit down. Do you want to hear about all the art they took in over fifteen years and nothing bad happened between them, about how they always seemed to hit a wall with it at the exact same time, that their energy levels for art or more or less any activity outside the house matched surprisingly well, in spite of the age difference? (Did you forget there was an age difference?)

Or do you want to hear about how he sometimes wouldn't entertain what she had to say about art, or at least when it came to what she thought about his relationship to art, or different ways people could put art into the world, because he was the artist and he understood art and the art world more fully than she did? Do you want to know how many times they watched *30 Rock* in bed and laughed and laughed and nothing bad happened between them, do you want to hear how many times she watched *The Walking Dead* on her iPad after they went to bed, because she was postmenopausal and didn't sleep as well as she used to, before he decided this was a problem for him? Do you want to hear about their easy division of labor, how he, more or less, did the bills and the fixing of things and the vacuuming and the occasional evacuation of bats and how she, more or less, did the shopping and the dishes and the laundry, or do you want to hear how he sometimes pointed out how this dish or that pan wasn't clean enough, or how he adamantly denied that she did 95 percent of the laundry? (Do you even want to get into a discussion of gender roles here, or can we accept that they both chose chores they minded least or maybe even liked?) Do you want to know how many summers they went camping at least once, how much she loved sleeping next to him in a tent, or do you want to know that one day he decided he didn't like camping so much anymore, too much trouble, she didn't help enough, or quite the right way, even though she pitched the whole tent herself that one time (even if it was just to prove a point), and that it didn't seem to matter all that much to him that she might have liked to go camping again? Do you want to know about all the weekends in cute Airbnbs, starting with the very first one, so soon after they started dating, how easy it was, how much sex they had that time even though they were tired, or do you want to hear about how he came to resent that she wasn't the primary planner of these Airbnb excursions, even though there was maybe a reason she wasn't the primary planner of these Airbnb excursions, maybe because he didn't like the Airbnbs she chose, and sometimes when he didn't like the way she did things, she just stopped doing them? Do you want to hear about how these weekends, usually one or two a year, were the totality of their vacation time each year over the course of their marriage? Do you want to hear about how great their honeymoon in Taos was, how they had sex in Taos every day, all the art they saw, the food they ate, horses they rode, hikes and mud baths they took, or do you want to hear that their honeymoon was the last real vacation they took, that she let it be known many times how much she wanted to travel with him to Europe, or to an island somewhere, but due to budgets and time limits they really only ever went to see their families on vacations, which, yeah. Maybe it's all boring, or maybe she doesn't know the half of it, maybe she's been in denial about what's been going on in her relationship the whole time, maybe the whole time it's been a story of quietly seething resentment. Do you want to hear about how many times they never fought, how they never really fought at all until after it was over? Do you want to hear about the fights that happened after? Because there were a whole bunch of those.

Punks Would Punch You in the Face

For an early date, he invited her to a punk show with his punk friends and in her mind, she saw their relationship end right there, a bunch of punks sizing her up, her safety pins were in her sewing kit, not her face. There were still punks in 2003? Did she even own one black item of clothing anymore? She likes color. Color isn't punk. So she passed on the punk show, thanks but no thanks to being judged by the punk friends as being unsuitable for their punk lifestyle. She had no illusions about being cool in any universe, punk, hipster, cheerleader, whatever the hell any bunch of people thinks is cool. Her overall music vibe was best represented by Billy Joel. There may occasionally be some vaguely edgier additions to the baseline Billy Joel aesthetic, like Ben Folds, but she comes from Billy Joel. Her taste can be graphed from Elton John to Billy Joel to Ben Folds. Punks would punch you in the face for saying you love Billy Joel. She liked her face.

The punk friends turned out to be a young arty married couple with an awesome little kid who would in a relatively short time become some of her favorite people on the planet. So she doesn't know shit, sometimes.

Good Firsts

They had been together for about nine months when New Year's Eve rolled around. The so-called punks still lived in his hometown of Kalamazoo, but the four and a half of them had already spent a fair amount of time together in one city or the other, and so the punks came to Chicago for New Year's and they all went out for sushi and came home and stayed up talking and laughing and playing games and watching movies and sleeping in a big stupid pile, which meant that because there was no guest room you grabbed a blanket and went to sleep whenever or wherever you wanted, middle of a game or movie. This was the first of many best New Years spent with the so-called punks. This was the first of many best times spent with the so-called punks. This was her first New Year's with a boyfriend, first New Year's ever as a couple hanging with another couple. There were a lot of firsts that year. Good firsts. First guy to tell her he loved her (okay look, there are one or two other examples where those words went out there, but try to trust that we can disqualify those), first guy she'd been with for nine straight months, first guy she brought home to her dad's for Christmas. First guy she would actually have brought home to her mom in over a decade, if her mom were still alive. Both her parents are now long dead, so yay, no one in her business now that it's over.

Your Trip

She's been invited as part of a tour of Rwanda to meet different groups of Rwandan students interested in reading and writing. She's in Rwanda looking over the mountains in Kigali and eating tree tomatoes and home-cooked meals and working with young Rwandan writers and meeting Rwandan artists and musicians and performers and staying in a swanky hotel that has one of those bug netting things over the bed and a spa bathroom and a balcony in front and a landscaped patio in back, with an outdoor shower even. She hasn't left the country in over twenty years (see also no vacation), not counting a couple days in Montreal, not to slight Canada as a country, she just has not left the continent in a very long time, and now she's in Africa, a continent she hoped to see but never imagined she would, doing something that she loves, no less, but she's also in couples counseling, and she's away again, for nine days, and she wishes so many times that her husband could be with her, to see the art, see the landscape, meet the people. Be with her. They FaceTime when they can, though time zones are problematic, and a couple days in she says *I wish you were here*, and he says *It's your trip*, and she knows he's saying he's happy she's having this experience but she wants him to say *Me too*, and then she says she's been feeling a little sad, and he asks why, and she says *I miss you*, and he doesn't say it back.

Answers to the Question *What Are You Thinking About*

2003–2012: Art.

2012–2017: Windows.

She always felt relieved that these were his answers because the answer was never *Someone else* or *I'm not happy* until it was.

Forgetting

Once upon a time maybe six or eight years into the marriage, at her dad's house in Iowa, the couple was on the sunporch (which serves as a guest room when all the guest rooms are filled with miscellaneous siblings and family members), watching TV on the foldout sofa bed, which was lumpy, as foldout sofas often are, though this one was lumpy in an inexplicable way, since it's a decent-quality mattress with a nice quilted pillow top. There's a hill on one side of the mattress, around where one's shin might be, depending on one's height. The husband was on the lumped side of the bed, switching channels, and landed on some program that caused him to ask the wife what she thought about the idea of an open marriage. It wasn't even some sexy late-night cable show, it was some random show and maybe there were two women on the screen, maybe two women and one man. Sisters and a brother. Coworkers. Tina Fey and Amy Poehler as Sarah Palin and Hillary Clinton. Anything from *South Park* to *The Wire*. Some random and unsexy moment, involving whatever series of thoughts gets a person from *South Park* or *The Wire* to open marriage. Almost all of the details of the story are long forgotten except for the feeling she experienced upon hearing his question, which was along the lines of having been smacked in the head, and her response was more or less *If that's what you want you can go get it with someone else*. No lengthy conversation on this topic followed. The husband was only curious about her thoughts, and assured her he only wanted to be with her. The wife's thoughts on this always fell to whatever floats anyone's marriage boat was all fine by her but the boat she floated into this marriage on was a two-seater. *Good, the wife said, I will set about forgetting this conversation ever happened.* Or something like this. Or maybe she only thought this. But you know, when you get smacked in the head, even if you don't have a headache the next day, it's hard to say what the lasting effects are. You could have a brain injury.

States

She had an idea about having sex in all the states. So they did that, they did it in Illinois, they did it in Michigan, they did it in Indiana on the way to Michigan, they did it in Wisconsin, Iowa, and Nebraska, they went west and did it in New Mexico, Nevada, California, Oregon, and Washington, they circled back to do it in Oklahoma, they did it in Missouri or Kansas, one of those, they took it down to Texas, and then they did it back east in Maryland, Delaware, Ohio, Pennsylvania, and New York. Also Canada one time. They could have done it in Massachusetts, twice, but they didn't. They might have done it in West Virginia but she can't remember. He told her she was *sexmerizing*. They did it in the woods of New Mexico and they did it on the California Zephyr, and they did it standing up and sitting down and sideways and on beds and sofas and floors. They tried to do it in all the rooms of their house but usually ended up in the bedroom maybe because that's where the lube was. They never stopped doing it, but we won't say it was as often as they did the first few years. They did it the night before he left.

Good Mother

While they were still dating, she loved driving down to see him in Pilsen from her apartment in Ukrainian Village. She'd never been a fan of driving, ever, but she had come to be a fan of having a car. The drive south to Pilsen from Ukrainian Village was low-key enjoyable; she'd listen to BEZ, or a CD, lately that Flaming Lips he left in her car, and it's a half hour of anticipation of being with her new love, sitting on his sofa, talking for an hour or two, making out for an hour or two, maybe doing more than that for an hour or two in his full-sized bed, spending the night spooning.

I don't think you'd be a good mother.

This is a thing he said, some months in, maybe three, maybe six? Does it matter? Is there a time to ever say this? It's a thing he said in his bed, with her on the side up against the wall, and there was some conversation prior to this statement, she's pretty sure, it wasn't totally out of the blue, but look, no matter where this comes in the conversation, any conversation, it's not a thing to say. It's not a thing to say.

She said—*something*, she remembers that much, and she remembers having some strong feelings about what this might mean for them as a couple. Like forget whether or not they'd have kids, only that he would think this and then say it out loud. Forget whatever kind of mom she thought she'd be. She had her own doubts, didn't need anyone else throwing theirs into the mix. She wasn't a pioneer of doubts about one's maternal capabilities, she was good with kids, she thought, had a lot of experience working with kids, loved kids, but would she be good with her own kids, kids she didn't get to send home to someone else at the end of the day, who is so sure they'll be good moms before they do it for real, liars, nobody. Maybe there are no good moms.

Was there some reason she didn't say *Okay, well since you think this, and you know you want kids, I guess bye?* She's sure, because she didn't say that, because she didn't leave, that she was somehow able to make him see that this was maybe not a thing to say (though she had no mind to try to convince him about her potential parenting skills because fuck that) and he backtracked, said it wasn't what he meant, apologized, never said a thing like it again and apologized many more times over the years, during which time the kids conversation evolved from his *I want them* to her *I'm open* to their *Let's table this*, where it stayed, but it was still a thing that was out there, a thing she would always know that he had one time thought.

A Thing

She started to make the bed wrong. Maybe she always had. It bothered him now. The fitted sheet always came up at the top. *I can't reach down there any better,* she said. *Just try,* he said. *I am trying,* she said.

Other Things

A few times after a long flight home from a long work trip she came home to find the gas tank on empty. She always asked him not to, it made her anxious. He said *There's always enough to get to the gas station.*

A few times after a long flight home from a long work trip she came home to find a sink full of dirty dishes. It made her wonder if he was resentful that she traveled, but she didn't say this. She asked him not to next time. He said he'd try.

A few times after a long flight home from a long work trip, he was late to pick her up at the airport. It made her sad. She said nothing.

A Worse Thing

Some years in, ten or more, he began asking her to prove things, in casual conversations. She'd say *I read this article that said such and such*, and he'd say *That's not true. Where did you read that, show it to me*, and she'd say *I don't like when you talk to me like that.* He usually indicated frustration when she pointed this out, tried to dial back talking to her like that, but the conversation usually wrapped up after this.

Maybe the Worst Thing

He didn't read her most recent book. He read the first two stories and he left it open on the coffee table on top of a stack of *New Yorker*s, which was how he always left his place in books, and it stayed there and stayed there and stayed there and time went by, a month two three months, the open book stayed there for three months four months some long amount of time and she told herself some stories that he didn't read as much as he used to which was true but it was fucking dedicated to him this book and it stayed there and stayed there until the cover read *Your Husband Does Not Want to Read Your Book* at which time she couldn't look at it anymore so she put a bookmark in it and put it on the shelf and it wasn't looked at or mentioned again by either of them. But look, maybe he had his own list of things. Maybe on his list of things was *She never comes by my shop to see what I'm working on.* This was known to be on his list, actually. Who is she to say it's not the same? Maybe he didn't read her book because she didn't come to his shop and this is just how it goes, things not being said.

Emergency

Filling out forms at couples therapy round two, she notices that her husband puts his sister down for his emergency contact. She doubles over into tears. *Put me!* He seems startled into submission, scratches out his sister's name, puts hers in.

This Story Will Be a True Story

This story is a story and this story is true. This story will change and then it will change again. This story will change before it is done being written, it will change after it is written. All these things are true.

Counseling Again

After the husband moves out, the wife spends the summer crying hard and being baffled about why someone ends a good marriage and whether or not the marriage was actually good even though she had always thought it was good and more or less is only trying to get through the day on the off chance that at some point there will be less crying and then someday maybe no crying, about this topic. (There will never be no crying. There will always be crying now. *Crying's where it's at,* a friend says one day, and the wife appreciates the great truth of this.) The wife can no longer bear to see the husband for any reason, coming to get stuff from the house, take the dog out, whatever, she can't see the husband without bursting into tears. Sometimes she hides when he comes by, sometimes she doesn't, sometimes she can avoid starting a conversation, sometimes she cannot help starting a conversation. They have a few conversations that are emotional on both ends and which indicate a certain willingness to try to understand what really happened that she hasn't yet seen from the husband. Somehow this ends up with them going back to couples counseling, with a new couples counselor. Not to reconcile. We won't say they're trying to consciously uncouple, but they aren't not. The wife wants to understand what happened, and the husband has come to understand, or to seem to understand, that he had been abrupt in ending the marriage, though he doesn't seem to regret it. He is still exploring with the client. He hasn't gained a willingness to work on the marriage, but he's gained a willingness to talk about the marriage. There is some concern on the part of the wife that the husband is motivated by his exploration with the other person in some way and not his genuine willingness to do some of the work he didn't do in round one. He has hinted that things are not perfect, that he's far from setting up house over at this other woman's mansion. The wife doesn't want details but says *And what's the common denominator there, ya think?*

I know, he says.

She is trying to take his words at face value, though they are both known to leave words out.

It emerges that he now takes the client to the restaurant she considered their special-occasion place, that farm-to-table place on an actual farm, chalkboards and drip coffee, fresh baked goods and picnic tables by a stream, string lights and posies in saltshakers, little kids in tiny handmade cardigans and tiny wellies on tiny bridges feeding ducks. How does someone do that? How does someone go to a place that was their place with someone else? Their place with *tiny cardigans*? Go find your own place. Does the client even know it was their place? *This is the woman I love.* This is what he says when she tries to point out that it's not nice to seduce other people's husbands. *You don't get to say shit about the woman I love.*

Sure I do, she says.

So the couple goes to a second shitty couples counselor and they talk more about it and they both cry, a lot, and sometimes it feels like progress is being made, that useful information is emerging, other times, it feels like her teeth are being pulled out one by one with a pair of pliers, and that if the second shitty couples therapist praises the husband one more time for showing up to couples therapy after they've already split up, there will be screaming, and if there is screaming, there will be no end to screaming, there will only be screaming forever and ever after.

Tickets

They'd been dating for six weeks, two months? He was already talking marriage. They weren't rushing into sleeping together, partly because of his Christian idea of waiting until after marriage (he'd only been Christian for a few years, so he hadn't been waiting his whole life), but somehow he overcame that obstacle, and they actually planned it more or less, or at least that he would sleep over at her apartment for the first time, and what that probably meant, so by that point he'd come to believe that he could align his having sex with his Christianity. Anyway, her new boyfriend/future husband brought pajamas and a toothbrush, which maybe doesn't sound sexy to you but was very sweetly sexy to her, and they started sleeping together, often, and then one day they were in her bed and he got up out of the bed to go to work, or somewhere, and he was like *So you know if we get married I'll be the head of the household*, and here we'll let you choose from her responses, which might be a) *AHAHA-HAHAHAHAHAHA*, b) *Dude, I know it's only been two months but I know you have met me*, c) *Yeah, no*, or d) *all of the above*. This was the extent of this conversation in that moment, but a few days later when he came to understand that she'd never become a Christian, he broke things off. She brought meat loaf in a glass pan to his apartment for dinner, they had the breakup conversation, she took the leftover meat loaf and the pan with her, got to the corner, threw the pan with the meat loaf still in it onto the ground, sat on the curb, cried, hoping he'd hear the pan break/her crying and come out and fix it. He didn't.

That night she went to a meeting and talked to her friends afterward, standing outside a church in Wicker Park. She knew that this was a kind of progress for her, that she was willing to let go of someone she loved over her own spiritual beliefs, which had been fuzzy over the years to say the least, and occasionally felt like a crisis to say the most. The recovery program she's part of is considered to be a spiritual one, even though it's one where you get to decide on a god of your own understanding, and if that happens to be Jesus or a whale with wings or a deflated Mylar balloon or no god at all, it's up to you, except she wants to have more faith in her faith, basically, but she doesn't, she has always wanted to know exactly what it is and how it works. But no amount of obsessing over this has ever gotten her there. There was a time in her young adult life when she would have converted for a dude she loved, she'd have converted all her ounces to liters, she'd have converted her dollars to donuts, she'd have converted her entire self. But by the time of the Christianity proposal, she had come to want to keep more of that self, to know that self a little better, at least enough to choose a fuzzy god of her own misunderstanding, at least enough to know that if she was going to be part of a white heteronormative marriage, she wasn't going to add any further notions of patriarchy to that, and so she let Christian dude go, and it was painful, but this was only about two months in, she knew she'd live, she had before, and then the next day he came over to say he wanted to stay together, that she was amazing and he loved her and he didn't want to lose her, and she reminded him she wasn't going to be a Christian, and he said he understood, he said *I'm asking you to take me back*, and handed her tickets to two different concerts in the coming months, and all she could think was, You really think we're going to be together by the time these shows come around?

His Birthday

The wife goes on a work trip. The husband sometimes whines a little bit when the wife goes on work trips, sweet complaints of missing her. The wife always tells him to go out with friends, make plans. *Or you know, come with me.* He's done that once in the ten years she's had the job. Wait, maybe twice? On the one or two visits, they cover what's to be done in Palm Springs to his satisfaction, a gallery or two, a hike in Joshua Tree, Noah Purifoy's outdoor museum, though in her view maybe what's actually to be done in Palm Springs is to hang out and relax with a book by the pool while she's in class and then hang out with the wife and her friends at the end of her workday, for a few days. *We can't afford it, I can't take off work, someone has to stay with the dog,* whatever. These things are true. So once in a while he'll go to a movie with a friend during those ten-day trips while she's away, maybe a gallery show, otherwise he mostly goes to work and comes home and stays up late watching TV until she gets home. Anyway, this last time she's away, the client and two other newer friends take the husband out for a belated birthday dinner.

What do you think about my friendship with her? the husband asks the wife.

I'm glad you have a friend. I think she likes you, she says.

The wife is glad the husband is going out. She jokes with her coworkers that her husband is out with his girlfriends. One of them is seventy-five. One of them is married. One of them has a crush on the husband. She isn't worried. Her husband loves only her.

Food

The client often cooks lunch for him while he's working on her house. The wife hears about this later.

Coffee

The wife crosses the river to Beacon to meet a friend for coffee. The husband and the wife occasionally cross the river for this or that, there are more shops and galleries and restaurants across the river, it's something to do, but mostly for coffee they stay on their side of the river. So anyway the wife has coffee across the river with the friend and then in walks the husband and the client, and the wife feels something she doesn't like and then she lets it go because no way, not her, not him, not me.

She Brought a Big Fish

The husband and wife have a movie night for a few friends. Some of them bring snacks. The client brings a giant cooked fish in a baking dish. It's not a movie snack and they've already had dinner but whatever. *Wow,* the husband says. *Look at that,* he says. The wife nods. The client takes her shoes off and splays herself on their floor like the house belongs to her, looks at the husband moony-eyed. There's nothing subtle about it. The wife resists an impulse to snuggle up to her husband, stare down moony eyes. They watch the movie. The movie ends. The husband walks the client and her girlfriend out to their car across the street. The wife tries to think of one time the husband ever walked anyone from their house to their car across the street. The wife watches them from behind the blinds, like something might actually happen between them in front of their house. Nothing happens between them in front of their house. The wife is acting like a dope. Her husband has always loved her madly. The husband comes back in. *She brought a big fish, wasn't that nice?* She wishes to renounce this part of herself. It flares up so rarely that she does not consider it a critical part of her character, but when it does, it can come with an intensity that makes up the difference.

Festive

A movie she co-wrote, based on her first novel, is premiering at a film festival on Nantucket less than a month after her husband moved out. The husband was supposed to drive. She is not confident about driving herself to Nantucket, has no plan for where to stay. Her screenwriting partner, the director of the film, calls to tell her that his mom has died. Condolences are offered, sadness shared. He asks about her plans for Nantucket. She says she doesn't think she can afford it, doesn't have a hotel room, has plans to stay home and be sad. The director tells her he and his wife are on a cheap flight, she really should come, maybe there's room in an Airbnb. *You shouldn't miss it,* he says.

Okay, she says. *I'll try.* She hangs up, makes travel arrangements easily and quickly, calls her friend back.

Excellent! he says. *I look forward to crying all over Nantucket with you.*

The final cut has come out beautifully. One of the story lines in the film is a crumbling marriage and an affair. It's quite a different story than her own, it's actually the wife who strays, for one thing, and was written many years prior, but not having seen it for a while, it bites.

The film is well received. Director friend throws a beautiful dinner at a restaurant afterward for the cast and some of the crew, many of whom are friends. Toasts are made under twinkly lights, heartfelt gratitude for the collaboration and opportunity. There is crying on Nantucket. The wife knows most of the people at the table at this point, but there's a couple across from her who she's only met briefly, and now the wife is crying at the table. *My husband left,* she says.

I'm so sorry. I was with someone for nine years before we met, the man across from her says, gesturing to his husband next to him. *I was devastated when it ended. It gets better.*

The following afternoon, the wife spends part of the day wandering around Nantucket. Windows make her think of her husband. Ones he'd approve of, ones he wouldn't approve of. She can tell the difference now between good glass and bad glass, cannot call to tell him about the good thick wavy glass in the lovely old wood multipaned windows, or the bad flat glass in the metal replacement windows that seems like it will shatter if you look at it sideways. One of the co-stars of the movie has a shack on the beach, invites everyone over for drinks at sunset. There's a party on the beach in Nantucket at sunset celebrating her movie.

The other co-star offers the wife counsel. She's been married for a long time, but knows from a bad breakup.

I'm good at this, she says. Her friend confirms.

Let yourself cry all summer, she says. *In September, no more crying. Get yourself back out there. You have everything going for you. Allow yourself a setback around Thanksgiving, the holidays.*

Whoa, that's hard-core, the wife says. *You're not fucking around.*

She's not, her friend says.

Trust me, she says. *You'll get through this.*

Say a Prayer

They'd been together for eight or nine months; he wanted to be officially engaged before they moved in together, but there was a listing in the *Reader* for a place off Division for $900 a month. They almost blew it off at the last minute because it was freezing and maybe they were rushing things, but it was $900 for a three-bedroom, c'mon.

The landlord was an aging hippie, Chicago-neighborhood style. He'd lived on that block his whole life. The front door of the apartment opened into the foyer; at first glance it seemed like one of those typical long Chicago apartments, a room in the front, rooms in the middle, a room in the back, the Chicago version of a railroad but with doors. He walked them to the living room, in the front. *The heater's in a weird place,* he said. *Built in 1901.* There was a small room off the living room, a perfect office, a place for her desk right in front of the window. Back through the living room to the foyer, the landlord opened another door into a long, narrow room. *This is an odd room, there used to be a wall in the middle here, there's no fixture, this outlet doesn't work, I don't think.* Silently, they pictured their stuff there, maybe an office for him, maybe a guest room, maybe a kid's room. In the kitchen, the landlord said *There aren't really any cabinets or counters. I built these shelves but that's it. Also this is the only bathroom,* he said, opening a door within the kitchen. *I know right off the kitchen isn't ideal.* At the back of the apartment, another bedroom was long and wide, windows on two sides, room for both their ancient dressers, a big bed, maybe even a chair. *There's a big crack in the ceiling up here,* the landlord said, *you see this, right?* Was he expecting them to negotiate at this point? So far all they knew was he was showing them rooms upon rooms and he wasn't done yet. An open doorway at the back of the bedroom led into another small bedroom, with another window. Maybe it was a baby's room once, since the only way to enter it was through the larger bedroom. *There's no closet in this room, though.* The couple was communicating psychically at this point. They knew that could be the closet. The landlord took them up a small staircase to an attic the size of the entire apartment downstairs. *It's unfinished, though. Well, there is a room in the front, I'll show you, maybe you could use it for something.* The brick was noticeably leaning outward toward the ceiling on the south wall. This was the only flaw the landlord didn't point out, the only one that seemed truly problematic long-term. Would this amazing, quirky old house literally fall down on top of them? It had been standing for a hundred years! In back of the house, there was an upper deck and a lower deck and a fully landscaped yard. *I built this, did all the landscaping myself. Those are rosebushes, lilacs, lilies.* There was also a big shade tree and a small curving path to the wooden gate that led to the back alley. *It's a shared space. I use the storefront space for a studio but I live in my brother's building next door.* They told him it was the first place they'd looked at, but they liked it and they'd think about it and get back to him soon. They giggled in the car as soon as they left.

Was that too good to be true? Could this be this easy? How can we only look at one apartment? Is it too soon? Let's sleep on it. No, let's say a prayer. They looked at one apartment. When she first got to Chicago, she hadn't even looked at her first one at all when it was offered to her by a friend. Two bedrooms and a back porch? I'll take it, thanks. New York apartment hunting had never been less than a nightmare. Maybe in Chicago this was how it always was. Maybe it was meant to be. Did she believe in meant to be? She did not. She believed in what was, and what this was seemed pretty darn sweet. Maybe they'd get married in the backyard in the fall. They were giddy. They said a prayer. *God, help us make the right decision, let us know if this is the right thing.* God didn't answer back, but they moved in anyway, and got married in the yard anyway, and no one wondered what was right for a long time after.

Just Lean Forward

She is not a country girl. She's a city girl. She's the city girl next door. She likes the outdoors but she is not outdoorsy. She loves camping for sleeping under the stars in the tent, for coffee made over the fire in the morning, for reading in the hammock in the afternoon, for dinner by the fire in the evening. But she's a city girl. She loves having a patch of grass, or a back porch, the tiniest of her own outdoor space, in the city. She loves walking, in the city. She loves walking on the beach or in the woods too, but not as much if you're going to call it hiking. If there are hills involved, she does not love it as much.

Early on, when he was still her very new boyfriend, probably right after that word was introduced, which was day one, now that we think about it, anyway, she and her new boyfriend/future husband went to a secret beach in Michigan, and to get to the secret beach you had to climb down a dune that was at a ninety-degree angle to the beach. Okay, maybe eighty. An angle sufficiently steep that going down it didn't seem like an option at all. Something that looked more to her like a cliff than a dune. You can't slide down a ninety-degree cliff dune. This wasn't a secret beach, it was an unreachable beach. The punk friends were already waiting at the bottom, setting up their blankets. The girlfriend/wife-to-be looked around for a gentler slope. There wasn't one. This was it. This was the difference between them. She liked a flat beach, a flat hike. A cliff dune was nothing to him. It was over.

I'm a city girl. I can't do this. I'm going to fall.

You won't, the new boyfriend/husband-to-be reassured her. *I'm right here. Just lean forward,* he said.

That makes no sense! she said. He held her hand. She wiped away a few tears. She leaned forward. Ish. They got down the dune.

Faith No More

At the beginning, sometimes on Sunday she'd go to church with him, but after a while he didn't feel like driving all the way uptown to where his church was, or he wasn't in the mood, and she started hearing less about it, the church, or Jesus, or anything much at all about his faith, not that she ever heard a lot about it, thankfully. They did have conversations about their spiritual lives, but they didn't argue about it because they didn't argue about anything ever. One day, frustrated with some inconsistencies in his religion, she put forth some of her low-key ideas about god, something to the effect of *Whatever it is it isn't me*, and he said *I think I like your faith better than mine this week.* For some time after this, he said little more about the subject, and then one day about a year into the marriage, some fundamentalist right-winger said something on TV that he didn't like, and he got pissed and said *I renounce Jesus!*

He meant to be funny, but he meant it. What led him to Christianity in the first place had been something like an offer of clarity, which slowly seemed to emerge for him outside of that institution. Some years later he'd say he didn't believe in god at all.

Whose Life

The husband and wife opened their home in Chicago for a going-away party for a friend. The husband wasn't a huge fan of parties, was maybe not as social as the wife, but was agreeable. The wife had party parameters, but she was a fan. She liked having people over. An ideal party was a group of close friends who all knew each other. If there was a backyard, or a grill going, all the better. She also enjoyed throwing a bigger party, but could get stressed about mixing different pockets of friends. In this case, she felt like the pressure was off, since it was more about offering the space than hosting. Snow began to fall as guests arrived, boots and jackets began to pile up by the door. Some guys arrived with instruments, a cello, a guitar. They set themselves up by one of the living room windows, started playing some kind of low-key jazz. The party was going. Giant flakes of snow fell behind the musicians; the wife scanned the room, people listening, talking, enjoying. It was a scene from a movie. It's a thought she had often.

Look at this, hunny. Whose life is this.

Her husband put his arm around her. *It's our life.*

They Got a Dog

Once they brought the dog home, sometimes it seemed to the wife like the affection got redistributed in such a way that the dog actually got some of what each partner had previously allotted to the other. Versus there's enough love to go around. There's enough love to go around, isn't there?

They Got a King-Size Bed

Was this it? Was this it, the beginning of the end? They were living in Texas and they needed a new mattress and the idea was that the queen had been a bit crowded with her, him (he's tall), and sometimes their eighty-pound dog. So they got a king, but the dog still found ways to make it crowded, and her husband was now literally farther away.

They Got an L-Shaped Sofa

Maybe it was this, was it this? They got an L-shaped sofa and they sat on different sides of it. He stretched out on the side that you're supposed to stretch out on and she stretched out on the other side. Her husband was now literally farther away in two rooms of the house.

They Moved Upstate

The number of breakups of couples who moved to their town in the last five years seems notable. Does this mean something? Does it mean they'd be together if they hadn't moved there, or does it mean they had to move there so that they wouldn't be together because they weren't supposed to be together but they didn't know it yet? Couldn't they have not been together somewhere more conveniently located? Without moving?

They Watched a Show Called *Divorce* on the L-Shaped Sofa

She had to remind herself that she wasn't superstitious. At some juncture of stepping over cracks and not opening umbrellas indoors, she stopped to realize she had never believed in superstitions. Her mother's back did not break. Her mother died of cancer, and she was pretty sure there was no corresponding superstition for that. But she had killed a character based on her dad in one of her novels, and then he died, and she wrote about infidelity in that same novel, which obviously killed her marriage as well. So she continued to carry on some ill-considered ideas about the power of her thoughts to create realities. That dad thing we mentioned above fucked her up a bit. For the duration of her marriage she avoided singing heartbreak songs too, as though this would somehow manifest actual heartbreak. Anyway, they went ahead and watched a show called *Divorce* on their L-shaped sofa and she thinks now maybe that was all too much.

Should They Just Have Gone Ahead and Gotten One of Those Long-Ass Dining Room Tables Too?

And sat at opposite ends like elderly married royals in a movie who quietly loathe one another, and be done with it?

Sex

Here's something they have in common, but not in a good way: it's their least favorite topic of discussion. She's willing to let you know that she has sex, that she and the husband have sex, less willing to get into the specifics of that. What is there to say? It's basic, to the extent that no one's asking for things the other one hasn't heard of, or isn't willing to try at least once. Basic sounds awful, but she doesn't mean basic like the kids say or like all they do is missionary or whatever and that's that, and they're both satisfied, or at least this is how it appears and this is what they tell each other about it. Their first few years together, there's a lot of it. More than she needs, frankly, but that's okay, she thinks, although she worries that it isn't, because he has a thing about wanting her to initiate more than she does, and she has a thing about not wanting to initiate when she's not in the mood, which she usually isn't as soon as he is, because they just had sex, you know, yesterday, and so most of the time he initiates. Time passes and they have less sex but still a couple times a week for many years, which is still frequent enough for her to not be inclined to initiate, and so most of the time he still initiates. Then more time passes and they're down to maybe once a week, but somewhere along this way he stops initiating and her way of initiating tends to be verbal, and not in a super sexy way, she's aware (this wife + efforts at sexy talk = comedy), in like a *Hey can we make time for this* way. She's never thought of herself as super sexy. Like if you think of her as super sexy, that's cool, and know that she doesn't feel bad about herself, she just doesn't think of herself like this, and it lines up with her not wanting to suddenly get on top of her husband, which is probably more like what he's hoping she'll do.

Maybe know this: as she gets older, heading into and through and past menopause, sex becomes painful at times. That's one small thing. Or, not small. This does not make her want to have more sex, nor does it make her stop having sex, but it does make her think she wants to have less sex, you know, if it's going to hurt. Also, she has the idea that it takes her longer to get there than it used to, and she has the idea that her overall desire is down. She tries to be honest with the husband about this, and he sometimes tries to spend more time getting her there and he sometimes doesn't. And since her husband is also reluctant to pursue this topic, who even knows what he's thinking about it. What she least wants to say is that she stops wanting to really kiss him. She loves his mouth so much, he has soft, full lips, and when they were first dating they sometimes made out on the sofa for hours at a stretch. She has memory in her body of the first time they kissed, of the very idea of the kiss going through the entirety of her before she finally told him he could kiss her if he wanted, because she couldn't wait any longer for him to read her signals. They still kiss. They don't make out too much now. When he comes down the stairs in the morning and smiles at her she still thinks, He's so cute. She wants to want to kiss him.

This Story Will Not Be the Entire Story

It will be a one-sided story. It will be a one-sided portion of a one-sided story. Hopefully a new, better story will take its place.

A Different Story

There could be a whole different story about her relationship to New York City, and maybe the world does not need another story set in/about growing up in/that is a gritty portrait of/that is a love letter to New York City. Probably not the latter. Maybe a reconciliation with. Anyway it's a different story. The point here is that she thinks of New York as one more of her many complicated parents who maybe could have done a better job but in the end all made her who she is, for better or worse.

I'm leaving! You didn't pay attention to me.

Eight million people live here, sorry not sorry.

I was a little kid. You could have at least hidden a few more exposed dicks.

We had bigger problems back then. You should be grateful. Didn't you always have a roof over your head? Did we not give you a shit ton of art and culture? Did you not go to musicals and concerts and Macy's Day Parades and all the museums, did you not go on class trips on the Circle Line, did you not go ice skating in Central Park, did you not see the Rockettes at Radio City and The Nutcracker *at Lincoln Center, did you not fucking stand on a stage at Lincoln Center when you were eight years old and sing in the goddamned opera?*

Okay but whatever I can't afford you!

Not my problem.

But you give other people rent-controlled apartments that fall from the sky! You like them better!

That's not true, I love all my eight million children equally.

You don't!

Hey I did the best I could. You're a grown-up now. Figure your shit out.

Everything We Need

So a few months after the husband moves out, when the fancy couple offers the wife their pied-à-terre in the East Village for a longer stay, she's down there with the dog and a suitcase the next day. *Welcome home,* they tell her. It is understood that this place to stay isn't forever, but it's also understood now that nothing is.

And then here comes her old buddy who has moved back to New York right at this same time after twenty years away, and he crashes in the East Village apartment with her and ends up staying, and the additional lodger is deemed just fine by the fancy couple. It's kind of what they do. They live in Jersey, they lend out their place in the city. Their very large two-bedroom in the city, who even knows how many square feet, one thousand, four thousand? The ceilings, with the original crown moldings, are high, maybe twelve feet, maybe twenty-five? The bathroom is a legit spa, from where we're coming. Anyway, her buddy is from Ohio, this guy is fully in love with New York, and it's a bit contagious; part of her is like *Okay but look at all the trash/it's so crowded/you don't understand, it's where I'm from, think of it as Ohio,* and he's like *Nobody stays in Ohio who has any sense,* she's like *I'm just saying I had to leave, sometimes you have to leave where you're from,* and he's like *Okay, so, you left, and now you're back,* and she's like *But I can't afford it,* and he's like *But you are affording it. Look at us. We live in the East Village and we have our bagel shop a block away and we have our deli down the block and we have a movie theater down the block, we have a meeting house two blocks away, our friends are here, we have CENTRAL PARK uptown, we have everything we need.*

When she was growing up, Central Park was not her favorite place. Central Park was about muggings and drug dealers and preppy killers and guys masturbating under trees. She tended to avoid it. She lived closer to Riverside Park, and it wasn't like they didn't have most of those same things over there too, but that's where she went sledding and played with her friends and ran away to, with nothing but a *Partridge Family* lunch box, that one afternoon in third grade because she was a lonely latchkey kid and no one understood her (she went home and no one was the wiser and having a roof seemed like a good swap out for being understood). Now her old buddy says *Let's get coffee and walk through Central Park with my kid today, let's walk through Central Park with our friends today,* and they walk through Central Park with the kid or their friends and they stop to watch performers, or they sit by the fountain, or they go down Poet's Walk, or they complain about the stupid new skinny buildings casting stupid shadows on Sheep Meadow but see that it's still so beautiful, and she sees it through different eyes, a little. A little. A little.

She Liked Having a Car

Once upon the late sixties a girl grew up in New York City walking places and taking subways and buses places and on special occasions taking taxis places and then the girl became a teenager who didn't want to learn to drive but then the girl became an adult who hoped to move away from New York City someday and so at twenty-five finally got a license so she could move impulsively to LA during rainy season, in which driving was a problem that could only be solved by moving impulsively back to New York City a week later. Then eight or ten years went by and she thought again of moving away from New York City and moved impulsively again, to Chicago this time, except she actually stayed and got a car and drove around and it was fine. It was mostly fine. Except people in Chicago tended to give directions by saying things like *It's at 2200 North and 600 West*, which was not helpful to someone not from Chicago, someone from New York City who didn't carry a compass around, someone who came from a city with numbered streets. She liked not having to schlep groceries home six blocks in the snow, not having to schlep laundry home six blocks in the snow. She liked being able to drive to Iowa to see her dad for a weekend whenever she felt like it. She liked being able to drive to her new boyfriend's place whenever she felt like it. She liked having a car. She did.

She Drove

On their first first date, that one where she thought they were friends and he thought it was a date, she drove. By this time, she knew how to get to many point Bs from her point A, and she drove them from the West Side of Chicago to Oak Park for a reading and they talked about buildings; there are a lot of warehouses and historic buildings on the way to Oak Park when you don't take the expressway. She did not take expressways.

Afterward, they went out with friends to that place where you can make your own s'mores, and the next day he called to ask her to go to a movie, that documentary about Andy Goldsworthy, the new boyfriend/future husband is an artist, and she likes art, and movies, and so they went to a movie and they were pretty much together after that (except for that twenty-four hours when they were broken up), and no mention was made of her driving or his driving, the conversation around driving at this point was limited to *Are we taking your car or mine.* And a lot of times they took her car, because her car was a car and his car was a truck. And it was always fine, until it wasn't.

He Drove

At some point they started going on more car trips, Chicago to Iowa to see her family, Chicago to Kalamazoo to see his family and friends, short enough drives that he didn't seem to mind doing most or all of the driving, and then they moved to Texas, so those were longer drives, drives in which he might have had extra time to start minding, and they drove back to the Midwest a good number of times over those three years that they lived in Texas, and one or two times they also drove to New York from Texas, and then after they moved to New York they often drove from there to Michigan and/or Iowa and back.

Driving in Texas brought her unanticipated challenges, challenges that caused not a few meltdowns, challenges including that in Austin, it isn't such and such hundred North and such and such hundred West, it's take 35 to 290 or 183 to Mopac, whatever the fuck that is, anyway these are expressways or highways or some other awful ways, and people in Austin made it out like there was no way around town other than to take highways, which isn't true, and/but, worse, even when her husband drove, it seemed like all of those highways had high cloverleaf loops to go from one to another, suddenly she had vertigo or fear of heights or something, because she didn't want to be in any car with any driver on any of those hellrides. It was during the Texas years that GPS became more of a thing, so she got herself one, which was life-altering. She had been crying for months about getting around and missing Chicago and her dad was so sick and so far away now and she didn't know what all else she was crying about, maybe it was all just menopause, but she got the GPS so at least she could get around. The husband was not a fan of GPS and didn't want to spend the money. He knew how to get around.

At some point, there was criticism of her driving. Even if it was subtle or vague, maybe it was just a sigh, he had a certain way of sighing that in this context seemed meant to indicate frustration, and she finally asked him to please not criticize her when she drove otherwise he was welcome to do all the driving.

So he did all the driving. They agreed to this. She was glad not to have to drive, and she was glad not to have to drive while being criticized. Or sighed at. She did not think he was a perfect driver either. She thought he was a good driver. She tried not to criticize, but if he got too close to another car, she would sometimes shriek. And he didn't care for that! She couldn't blame him because she is for sure a naturally jumpy person but she had actually prevented a couple of accidents by shrieking or yelling. One time she yelled but not soon enough to stop a minor accident from happening, which was undeniably his fault. She had tried to explain defensive driving to him in the past, but it seemed like he didn't believe in it. It seemed like he believed everyone would just do the right thing like he did or something. So what happened here was that he tried to right a wrong by doing a right, which in this case became wrong. You can't keep going if the person in front of you doesn't stop or slow down just because they were supposed to. You slow down. There was an accident. She was angry with him for a minute but he knew it was wrong and what can you do when you've just had a car accident and your partner has admitted they're wrong? You don't say, *Yeah, really wrong.* You just try to recover and be grateful no one was hurt.

Anyway this thing with him driving and her not driving went on for the rest of their marriage, and it seems now like it was a problem, like they had made this adjustment because it was easier than actually working through it, and that he was resentful that he had to do all the driving even though he said he wasn't, and that she was resentful that he hadn't made peace with it, or whatever. We don't know. It's a thing that became a whole big thing. That they stopped talking about.

Chicago

She loved Chicago more than she ever loved anything, or at least as much as she loved anything. She loved it in her body. She loved it in a romantic way. She loved it in that romantic way where you can list a million details about why you love a person but in the end it's not something there are exact right words for.

Leaving Chicago felt like a breakup. A bad breakup, one where you second-guess, where you only remember the good, a breakup where you always wonder a little if you should get back together. She thought she was ready. It wasn't a hard decision. Her husband had gotten a grad school fellowship in another city. It was a practical decision. It was her choice, one she made with her partner. Chicago didn't break up with her. She broke up with it. How she knew she loved her husband more than she loved Chicago is that she left Chicago for him. With him. For Texas.

Christmas Past

The wife was excited to make awesome Christmases with her husband. She set about filling his stocking each year with chocolates and kitchen doodads and other things he never got around to buying, like socks and t-shirts and underwear. She bought him graphic novels and art books and records for under the tree. She filled a stocking for the dog. Usually, they spent the actual day at the house with her dad and the extended family in Iowa. Those were some good times. The husband was your fun uncle who went all in on sledding and lawn games. If a Frisbee was tossed too far, he'd dive into a hedge for it with little hope of catching it. If there was something to do on a sled that you really shouldn't do, he would do it, standing up or lying down and aiming directly for a bump, and he would also go to the emergency room more than once on Christmas with a concussion or his chin split open. That time when he got the concussion he said a bunch of things that didn't make sense and in the emergency room the doctor put an X-ray of his skull on a lighted board and was that a crack on his skull and was her husband brain-damaged now, was this her new life, maybe this was what husbands and wives did for each other, maybe it all came down to a bump on the head.

Waco

One year, to save time, the husband and wife decided to fly from Austin to Iowa to see her dad for Christmas. Her dad's health was in decline. The wife had no love for air travel, had much anxiety around getting to her destination on time. Christmas Eve morning, they dropped the dog off with a sitter and flew to Dallas to catch a connecting flight to Cedar Rapids. The wife had been watching the weather reports, hoping that the weather in Iowa wouldn't mess up their travel. It didn't. The weather in Dallas messed up their travel. There was a snow-and-ice storm in Dallas. The wife had not thought to worry about the weather in Dallas.

In Dallas, the husband and wife boarded the plane for their connecting flight to Cedar Rapids. The plane pulled away from the gate, but there's only one de-icer at the Dallas airport because in Dallas the weather is warm. So the husband and wife and about two hundred other people waited on the plane nearly three hours to be de-iced, because the one Dallas de-icer broke down. There had recently been that JetBlue nightmare where people were stuck on the plane for so long they started eating their luggage and drinking their toiletries, or something, after which the NTSB dictated that if you're on the runway for three hours you have to return to the gate.

So the husband and wife returned to the gate, and waited and waited, schlepped around the Dallas-size airport from gate to gate hoping to catch either a different flight to Iowa or a flight back to Austin. The husband and wife waited and read books and magazines, watched a movie on her computer, but as the end of the day grew closer and closer, the wife started to seriously freak out about spending the night at the airport and/or having to fly on Christmas and finally convinced the husband they should rent a car and go back to Austin so they wouldn't mess up everyone's Christmas in Iowa by having them have to come get them in Cedar Rapids, an hour away, on Christmas Day, if they even got there at all. The husband did not particularly love sudden avoidable expenses like this, but had great patience with the wife's anxiety, so they dropped 300 bucks on a last-minute rental car, by which time it was creeping toward midnight, though the couple still thought the highway back to Austin would be fine, because there wasn't much more than an inch of snow on the ground. There was, however, an inch of ice underneath the inch of snow on the ground, and the highway system in Texas didn't seem to have that much more in place for ice removal than their airport did, so when they got into the car to head for the highway, Austin three hours away, the wife was so tired as to be near delirious as well as fearful of an accident. *It's all okay, we'll get a room,* the husband said, and they pulled off the road at the first exit, into the nearest motel, and went straight to sleep.

The next morning, near Waco on the way home, they were about to pull off the exit to a Starbucks for some holiday lattes, and a Texas Ranger pulled them over for speeding. Small and wiry, older, the brim of his Ranger hat way too big for his overly, aggressively tilted head, but no less sure of himself for it, on Christmas morning a Texas Ranger handed them a $150 speeding ticket like it was a present to himself and sent them on their way. At least they'd get to be with their dog. They ended the day with Chinese food. It won't be her last Christmas with her dad. It won't. It won't.

This Story Will Feel True

Is this story even true? It's meant to be true. Maybe this story is only as true as it feels to you. Does this story feel true to you? Then it's true.

Hole

After her dad died, he was cremated and his ashes put in an urn. There was no funeral, just a small family gathering at his home in Iowa, overlooking the meadow on the property where he'd spent half his life. They sat in a circle and shared Dad stories, heading to the cemetery afterward to put the urn in the family plot. A minister said a few words, asked if anyone wanted to volunteer to put the urn in the ground. *You'll have to lie all the way down on the ground to do it because it's a pretty deep hole,* he said. No one volunteered, but it wasn't a long beat before she found herself saying she'd do it. It felt like her task to do. She lay right down in front of the hole, took the urn with both hands, put it down in there and said *I love you* and *Goodbye.*

Sometimes now she wishes she could put her marriage in the ground and just say *I loved you* and *Goodbye.* But she doesn't want to bury it if it's still alive.

Reading

After her mom died, she still spent time and occasional holidays with her stepfather and, later, his new wife. But a series of events took place that coincided with the beginning of her career: her stepdad did a bunch of self-appointed detective work to determine whether the agent she'd chosen was *legit,* and he responded to the news that she'd gotten her first book deal, the very best news of her life, by saying *Congrats, sweetheart, now listen, you gotta fix yourself up.* Not even a period after *sweetheart.* One sentence.

When her third book came out, she and her husband traveled from Chicago to New York for some events and they met her stepdad and his new wife for sushi in Midtown near his office. She was giving a reading afterward and assumed they were coming. *No, no, we can't tonight,* her stepfather said.

Why not, her husband asked, with an edge to his voice that she might have had if she'd said anything at all, which she didn't, because she was busy turning back into a sullen, disappointed seventh grader who wanted the moment to blow over.

We have to go home and pack, her stepfather said. He was about to retire and they were moving south in a month or two.

It's an hour of your time, the husband said. Could also be worth noting here that for the last few decades of his life, her stepdad had been going to operas and concerts sometimes several nights a week. Operas and concerts that lasted more than an hour.

Can't, the stepdad said, unapologetically, adding that he'd read *a few* of her stories but didn't need to read any more because he was there when they happened.

So. Yeah. She wants so much to rant about that last statement here, now, still, in the future, but how much is there to say about something that makes no sense and yet still manages to be deeply hurtful.

The husband continued to push the stepfather, and the wife continued to slink under her napkin. *I don't understand. It would mean a lot to her.*

Her stepdad's final answer: *It's not going to happen.*

In the moment, she was just trying not to cry and waiting for her husband to drop it or for her stepdad to indicate some regret. The conversation felt like it lasted for an hour, but didn't amount to much more than however long it took to ask the waitress for Diet Cokes and for her to bring them. In later moments, the wife wonders if anyone has ever defended her so valiantly.

Marfa

For her fiftieth birthday, they went to Marfa. They took the dog and they stayed at a hip ranch where they slept in a vintage Airstream that had a deck with an outdoor bathtub, and an antelope came to play while they were there, and they went to all the galleries and saw all the art, and they ate at that awesome food truck, and they went to see the Marfa lights, but they only saw one, so they might have been mistaken (when people asked if they saw the Marfa lights they would always say *We think we saw a Marfa light*), and they went camping for a night and they hiked and crossed paths with some javelinas walking around and then they drove home, he drove them home, and it was a nice trip. But she wanted to go to Europe.

Swimming Holes

She fucking hated living in Texas. Hated it. She thought it might be okay, they'd spent time there before, but she came to hate it fully. To be fair to the people of Austin, they were as welcoming to her as the people of any other city she lived in. The husband and wife made friends, they were engaged in their respective communities. Austin and Chicago have this much in common for her. But she can no better explain her deep, abiding love of that city than she can her deep discomfort in this one.

Texas is about a lot of things, and yes, she's saying this as a non-Texan. Most of the things Texas is about she is not about, even though everyone loves Austin, we know. Look, it doesn't feel good to hate what everyone loves. Texas all around is about barbecue (dislike) and guns (super dislike) and Austin is about live music (don't all big cities have live music?) and sno-cones (okay, something she likes) and swimming holes.

She fucking hates swimming holes. Swimming holes are rocky and muddy and slippery and slimy and gross. She would have been happy without ever setting eyes on a swimming hole, but her husband had a fondness for nature of this sort. She has nothing against water. She loves water. She loves a waterfall, she loves a stream in the woods. She loves the ocean. The ocean is vast. It's mysterious. A swimming hole could be mysterious too, insofar as one might wonder who was murdered and tossed in there in a burlap sack.

Just before they left for New York, they went to one last swimming hole. The husband was now a Master in Fine Art, and having packed for the move, was eager to see anything he might have missed. The wife was recovering from a minor medical procedure and wasn't allowed to swim, not that she would ever swim in a hole, but the landscape of this special swimming hole was that it was surrounded by rock formations, steep, sharp, rocky rocks, one or two flat and wide enough to lay a towel or blanket on, most, not all of it precarious, footing-wise, which is another thing she doesn't care for in nature, precarious footing. So they were at the swimming hole with all the rock formations and absolutely no grass, no sand, no beach, and a shit ton of people, lying out on rocks wherever they could find a small perch, men and women and teenagers and toddlers, sunning and jumping off rope swings and floating on donuts and listening to loud and twangy music and eating and drinking and smoking. When you go to a swimming hole like this, unappealing to your personal sensibilities before you toss in a crowd, and some of them are smoking, and you're stuck on a cliff of jagged rocks, you're more or less trapped. You can't jump to the next rock. There is no next rock. Quickly, you reach a level of sadness over the swimming hole that is clearly, even to you, out of proportion to the very idea of crying over a swimming hole, which you would soon enough leave. You didn't move to the swimming hole. You went to the swimming hole for an afternoon.

The wife knew she was perhaps crying about other things, maybe she didn't even know what she was crying about, or if she was crying about more than one thing. She missed her dad, she didn't know what was next, moving is hard, who knows. Her husband was gentle with her about it, but there was something she couldn't touch that made her think he wished she'd just get over it. That she was wrong for not liking swimming holes. That she was wrong for having strong feelings about where she lived versus his absence of such. She didn't want to be crying about this being some major difference between her and her husband, not feeling the same way about swimming holes or Texas, but this felt closer to it.

She Did Not Hate Living in Brooklyn

Apartment hunting in New York had not improved in the sixteen years since she'd left. A bedroom was sometimes a room that their dog bed would not fit into. Real estate guys would not show up. The couple heard about a loft in Brooklyn that had a number of pluses. Good square footage, big windows, a view of the NYC skyline from the bedroom, a decent price. A loft! They went to see it one sunny afternoon and made a handshake deal; yes, they could wait a few months for some rehabbing. A few months went by, they went back to the loft one night to take measurements. At night, the street, a dark dead end under the BQE, looked like a place hit men met mobsters to take them out. The ceilings were lower than she remembered. There was a welding shop on the ground floor directly below the loft. The front window looked directly onto the BQE. Directly out the back window, in front of the view of the skyline, was a sizeable power plant. The two flights of stairs, with a short landing in the middle, were tall, narrow (if your heel was flush against the back of the stair, and you wore a women's size nine, the front half of your shoe would hang over the edge), and steep. *Exorcist* steep. No way could she do this every day with the dog. Were those stairs even wide enough for the dog's paw?

I can't do it, hunny. I'm so sorry. I feel so terrible for making us wait but I just can't.

It's okay, hunny, he said. *I was never crazy about it. I thought you liked it.*

They searched again in their price range, which was low, and they were moving to New York City and what were they thinking. She wanted her husband to have his dream of being an artist in New York, she suggested New York, they tried it for a few months, and she was ready to leave. She'd already been an artist in New York.

I want to go somewhere where it's easy, she said. She knew, knows, that's not really a thing.

Where will that be? he asked.

Kalamazoo? she said.

Nope, he said. *Michigan maybe. Someday. When we retire.*

The husband somehow found them a sweet one-bedroom walk-up in Clinton Hill. Nice moldings. Bay windows in front. Nice light. Weird neighbors who boil rats in the trash bin and raccoons staring into the windows from their fire escape. New York! Fireplace mantels in the living room and bedroom, decent ceilings, a small office area, bedroom somehow big enough for their king-size bed, kitchen you can cross in half a banana step, one small closet. But that's what carpenter husbands are for! He would build a closet and a bathroom cabinet and a window seat in one of the bay windows and the moldings on the window seat would match the moldings on the walls and it would look like it was always there. The wife had always wanted a window seat. The couple moved into the sweet Brooklyn apartment and the wife sat in the window seat and read books and watched sunsets and fireworks. They went to Prospect Park with the dog, movies at BAM, to the flea market up the street and the salvage shop around the corner. They found neighborhood spots, fancy donuts around the corner, fancy pizza down the street, a corner deli, a corner deli guy, and a corner deli cat. Brooklyn was perfect. In Brooklyn she could breathe, in Brooklyn she could see the sky, in Brooklyn there were people, but not so many that she wanted to shove them out of her way. The wife earned her living as a teacher and a writer and the husband worked as a carpenter six days a week to get the rent paid on their sweet Brooklyn apartment and his art studio that he had almost no time to go to. Their Brooklyn rent was double that of their entire house in Chicago. They lived there for a year and a half, and then they bought a house upstate.

The Big Box of Divorce

It started with an actual box. She and her husband were in Iowa for Christmas and her stepmom handed her a box, with the gentle advisement that she might not really want to look at what was in it. *It's your parents' divorce papers.* Except it's not just their divorce papers. It's Divorce Papers Plus. Probably as it could only ever be in her family. They saved stuff. If there was a scrap of paper with their name on it, it was saved.

Reason not to open the box: obvious?

Reason to open the box: she had no early childhood memories.

Reason she may have no early childhood memories: might be in the box.

She was obviously going to open the box.

She could probably have thought through whether it was the best idea to open the box on Christmas.

Initial inventory of the box:

Letters, newspaper articles, legal documents, a stack of recycled three-by-five notes (her dad was an early recycler and had a paper cutter he'd had since childhood, which he'd use to cut up paper he'd only used one side of) with her dad's handwriting on them, a crumbling rubber band around it, one pile of Christmas cards and other mail from mis-cellaneous friends, students, and family members between 1960 and '67.

In the letters category:

a) letters from her dad to his lawyer

b) letters from her dad to her mother's lawyer

c) letters from her dad's lawyer to her dad

d) letters from her mom to her dad, letters from her to her dad inside the letters from her mom to her dad

e) a letter from her paternal grandmother to (her dad?), we dunno yet, this grandmother was worse than a pill much of the time and she hated her mom (it was mutual) so she hasn't read it yet

f) letter from her mom's shrink to her dad

She spent about an hour with the contents of the box spread out on the gold carpet in the living room. She thought looking through the Christmas card pile would maybe be a gentle place to start, but there were other things mixed in there, including one anniversary card and one valentine from her dad to her mom with no personal sentiments included, both signed, simply, with his first name. After a tearful conversation with her stepmother she put everything back in the box and brought it back to New York and put it on a shelf in the basement.

Several months later, she remembered something she'd seen in the box that might be useful, and opened the big box of divorce again. She didn't find what she was looking for. But rereading the pile she was sure she'd already read in December, she was struck by the fact that she'd somehow already blocked things out.

Paint

Sometime after they moved into the house upstate, she went on a trip, she forgets where now, but she was away and her husband decided to surprise her by painting the bedroom. They had talked about painting it, they'd planned to paint it, she just didn't know he was going to paint it that particular weekend. The bedroom needed painting, and he was good at picking paint colors, and she had told him she wanted a pale pink, like paler than a pale eggshell pink, but pink, and he found a nice pink like this, and had the idea to do some type of wall treatment, a sort of thing where it looked like textured wallpaper, and he showed her the samples of what the textured paint would look like and she said sure. She liked to think of herself as pretty agreeable about décor choices because he had nice taste, and their taste lined up in many ways.

Would she maybe have been more risky with a bright paint color here or a bold fabric pattern on a chair there, if it were all up to her, sure, but they had a lot of nice art, and their sofa was blue, and she periodically made them a new quilt for their bed, which usually had many colors, and he loved her extremely not-perfect quilts with the seams that never quite lined up because she's not her mom and she's only going to rip out a mistake so many times (or more like no times). She brought her perfectionist game to other losing battles. The house wasn't lacking for color and she could work with a taupe wall here or there. But he wanted to give her a pink bedroom, and you have to love a guy for that.

And then she came home and only two of the walls were actually painted, that in itself wasn't a problem, or not at that point anyway, the problem was that it didn't look like the picture, and her initial response was definitely not the right one, probably something like *Oh*, and he had tried to prep her by saying he'd worked really hard on it but wasn't sure it had come out how he wanted, and *It's okay if you're not crazy about it*, and she wasn't crazy about it, she didn't hate it, but she didn't love it, at that moment it looked to her like fancy wallpaper that hadn't been lined up quite right, and it was that thing where you know someone's worked hard on something and you don't want to hurt their feelings but you're also not used to what you're seeing and so you say something, you say the worst possible thing.

Didn't you say you wanted our house to look like it could be in a magazine?

She made him cry.

Then they both cried.

Then they talked it through.

A lot of times when they talked things through it turned out to be about her mother. This particular time her mother was probably not involved. For all we know his mother was involved, or no one's mother was involved. Her husband wanted to do a nice thing for her, and he had ideas about having done so much work on the house already, some ideas we may revisit later, and it turns out that no matter how much gratitude you might feel and/or regularly express to your husband for all the ways he's rehabbed your home, it can all be completely offset by *Didn't you say you wanted our house to look like it could be in a magazine?* Later she grows to like the treatment, but the other two walls never do get painted.

Window Treatments

A few months before he moves out they take some measurements and go to look at window treatments. After a few years of living with the decrepit blinds that came with the house, the wife has begun to imagine how much better the room would look with the simplest of window treatments. Drapes here, linen shades there, pretty much anything. She has in the past made curtains for this apartment or that, but her sewing skills are modest and for the first house she owns, she wants an upgrade. So they go down to one of those shade stores on Route 17 in Jersey and they start looking at shades and the more she looks at the shades the more they all look exactly the same, and she wants him to decide and he seems to be vaguely irritated by her not wanting to decide, although he doesn't say that, but now she's also remembering what happened with the kitchen design, how disappointed he was with the amount of input she had provided in the design, which in turn hurt her feelings, because she had told him the things she wanted and he included most of them in the design, what they had room for anyway, and she was perfectly pleased with the design, had he not wanted her to be pleased? He said he guessed he wanted her to be more involved somehow, and she told him she didn't know how she could be more involved than she had been, and then his feelings seemed to be hurt. There are some shades in the shade store she really doesn't like, and she thinks the overall quality of most of them is not so great, the fabric scratchy, and they're all off-white or light-beigey, a pale leaf green is a wacky color in this store, not that she's looking for a bright color, we mention it only to emphasize that the lack of color in the shade store begins to take a toll on her, and it seems like they're there for an hour at the shade store on Route 17, which, if you haven't ever been, is a grim little stretch of the world on which to spend an hour, neither of them excited about window treatments, maybe even starting to resent the very existence of window treatments and bland choices and each other for reasons that are nebulous, given that this is an ordinary enough task. Maybe they're both just hungry and tired. They don't fight about it, what would that fight even be, but it feels like a fight without a fight, and the wife is finally like *I think I need to go home*, so they go home and share a Trader Joe's pizza and maybe watch an episode of something on Netflix and she goes upstairs at nine and he stays downstairs for a while and that's their Saturday night.

Collaboration

In couples therapy round two, he tells her he'd wanted to collaborate with her. That he wishes she'd have collaborated on the kitchen more. That he collaborated on the windows with the client in the client's house. The client's house has views of the river from the windows they collaborated on so the wife isn't sure why he hasn't fucking moved in there already. Maybe he has.

Is there more than one way to restore a window? Did the client suggest this type of wood over that? Did she suggest paint colors, stain colors in some way that was preferable, more invested, sexier than the way the wife considered paint colors? Did she help with cutting the wood, with sanding it smooth, replacing the glass, or the weights, or whatever the special word is for the weights? She probably memorized the word for the weights, is that what he wants? Did she help him put the restored window into the frame? Chop down the tree and cut the wood into two-by-fours? Just sit there admiring him and his work, bringing him gourmet meals she made, until it was time to fuck? Is that what we're really talking about?

The wife has collaborated before. She has collaborated with the husband and she has collaborated with others. She knows what collaboration means. She wants to know why collaboration is preferable to approval, to support, to faith in the work that the husband does. She wants to know when this became an issue. Did they not collaborate on everything? What is a good marriage if not a collaborative effort? Remember when they made those embroideries, the ones he drew and she stitched? She even chose the colors. They showed them in galleries and they even sold quite a few of them. They talked about doing more. She got the fabric out for him to draw on. It didn't get drawn on.

Doesn't This All Seem Pretty Common and Not Unusual or Even Awful at All in a Long-Term Marriage?

Like, when you think about all the things that could go wrong in a marriage, don't these people seem like they should make it?

This Level

Sometime in the last few months the husband and wife are in one of those Upper East Side galleries that's so fancy it's upstairs. It can't be bothered with the street, or the people who wander in off it. There are sculptures and paintings that remind the wife of the husband's work. The husband has not recently made work, is currently focused on his window-restoration business. *I think your work is on this level,* the wife says. *This is very good. It's not better than your work.* The wife anticipates a response here somewhere on a continuum between *My style of work isn't in favor right now* and *You don't know that much about it.* Things the wife almost never says: *I've been going to museums and galleries on the Upper East Side since I was eight years old. Maybe I don't have to be obsessed with art in the way you are, or have an MFA in art, to have valid thoughts about art. Maybe my experience with my art is relevant to your experience with your art. Maybe my ideas about how my work is, or should be, received in the world are relevant to your ideas about how your work is or should be or will be received in the world. Maybe the only difference is that my work* is *being received in the world.* The continuum of things the wife does say includes *You have shown your art in fucking museums. You have shown your art in so many galleries. You have walked into galleries more than a few times and said "I'd like to have a show here" and you've had a show there.* His response continuum from here diminishes all these achievements in different ways according to mood.

You might be right, is what he says.

The husband and wife have a long-running joke about his need to be right.

Sometimes I am! is what she says, with a tiny bit of cheer.

Marlboro

The husband wants to take a drive, have dinner in some other town, get out of their little city. They go to a saloon in Marlboro, but there aren't any tables free so they eat at the bar. It's not usually a problem, but sitting at a bar on this night, at this point, seems like a picture of the wrong versions of both of them. Service is extremely slow, or it feels that way to her. He wants to talk about being friends with the client again. They've had this conversation before. She has requested in couples therapy that he call a time-out on their friendship.

I can control myself, he says.

Do you hear what you're saying, though? she says. *I know you can control yourself.*

She was angry when I told her we couldn't be friends, he says.

Was she, the wife thinks.

She asked me, "Don't I get a say?"

Does it even matter the exact way in which the wife says *No*, or the exact way in which the wife points out that this person who is not in this marriage with them does not get a say?

It feels as shitty as anything that he's the one telling her this. She tries to make him understand this part of it too, but in a curious reversal, he suggests that there's something wrong with her for being closed about it. She should know now, she thinks, she should know everything she needs to know about how it's going to go from here. She should know.

I miss her friendship, he says tonight.

She should know now. She should know. Maybe she does know and doesn't want to.

Now she's crying at a bar. She didn't even cry at bars when she did drink. Wait, did she? She's sure she didn't. Probably. Not most of the time. She might have yelled at a bar a time or two or three.

They run into a friend on the way out, having dinner with his new girlfriend. There is no way not to say hi to the friend, no dodging out some back way, and no fake smiles to be mustered. Their friend suggests the four of them get together sometime. Their friend is in love. The wife knows this will never happen.

Trees Are Down

A tornado hits their town. Trees are down all over town, roofs are blown off historic buildings on their main street, small businesses destroyed, two lives taken. Her husband is extremely upset about the trees. He was already upset about the trees around town, the way they get trimmed into un-treelike shapes to accommodate electrical wires, or cut down entirely to accommodate one thing or another that isn't a tree. *Some of them were pulled right out by the roots. Some of the trees have been split open by the force of the winds, to reveal that they were rotten inside,* he says. *It seems like a metaphor.*

You think? she says. She does not think. *Which kind are we, are we a rotten tree?* You wanna do this game? Maybe your tree is rotten inside but your roots are tangled up in mine. My tree is a goddamn redwood. My tree is a motherfucking sequoia all the way through. A tree falls on his client's car. The husband moves out the day before the wife's birthday.

Given

It is a given that the dog will stay with the wife when the husband decides to move out. Then again, she thought it was a given that the husband would, upon announcing his plans to explore, move out, versus we don't know what exactly, becoming her roommate? But he did not take that as a given. Also a given is that the husband will continue to share the responsibility of dog ownership that they took on eleven years earlier when they brought him home. They have always split the dog walks. The husband walks the dog in the morning, the wife walks the dog in the afternoon. They take the dog to the vet together. The husband stays home with the dog when the wife travels every December and June. The husband moves out in May, takes the dog for one or two walks over the next few weeks, comes back to stay with the dog in June. The wife asks several times if he wants to make a custody schedule. The husband shrugs. *You know this is a responsibility, right? Not just like, a chair you don't mind if I keep?* Eventually, the husband will come around and see that it is in fact a responsibility, regardless of his seeming ambivalence about spending time with the dog. It's a curious thing, because she has witnessed the husband's relationship with the dog, saw, over the course of eleven years, that his love of and for the dog, his connection with the dog, was at least part of the equation of his recovery. So it seems like a given that the husband would, if not be sad about losing the wife, be very sad about losing the dog. Instead, she is sad about the husband not being sad about losing the dog.

Kalamazoo

Almost as soon as he moves out, she begins thinking about where she can move to next. It's what she does. She obviously can't stay in her town. But she's tired of moving. She loves her house. She owns it and she can afford it. She cannot quite picture being single in such a small town. She still wants love, someday, maybe. She's hardly eager to date. Like, ever again. But everyone knows everyone here. And it feels like a town full of couples.

Chicago is of course always first on the list, but having left, it feels like it could never be the same again. She does love LA, and work-wise that would make sense, but that's a no, she missed the change of seasons when she was in Texas. She could go back to the city, you know, if she had rent for that, but she doesn't. Also she doesn't really want to live there anyway. Also she loves her house. She owns it and she can afford it.

She has always loved Kalamazoo. It's a sweet college town, it's near Chicago, but her love for Kalamazoo is about her friends. The husband's oldest friends, the punks, have expanded into a solid core of people they have accumulated as dear friends over the years, in spite of not living there. They made frequent trips to Kalamazoo when they lived in Chicago, but those folks, punks that they are, would go on tour and come to Chicago as well, or Texas, or New York. They spent one Thanksgiving weekend in northern Michigan at a big cabin with the whole lot of them and their kids, one of her favorite Thanksgivings ever, talking and laughing and eating turkey and fondue and cake and playing games and singing songs and squeezing babies. She would have moved to Kalamazoo from the jump with the husband if he'd wanted to. (He didn't.) These people throw dinners and parties and bake for each other, they show up for each other when things are great and they show up when someone needs help and they show up when things suck. They're a community, something she's always dreamed of. And one she could jump right into. It isn't that community doesn't or can't exist in her town. It's that her Kalamazoo people have her heart.

But. Yeah. Right. So. That window probably closed. It may or may not matter that the husband is no longer close with some of these people. It's still too weird.

Still, she wishes he'd dropped her there instead of here.

Tinder Profile

I watch a shit ton of TV, especially late at night when I can't sleep, I watch horror movies and real housewife shows and peak TV shows and news shows but not the fake ones. I listen to whatever music I like. Some of it is not considered cool. Fuck you. I write a lot of books. I read a lot of books. I was married for fifteen years. We separated a year ago. I cry all the time still, I can't think about much of anything else. I hope you find that sexy. I don't go to the gym. Fuck the gym. I like flat hikes. I like bike riding where there are no streets. Do not ask me to bike ride in the city, I didn't do it for my husband and I won't do it for you. I eat whatever food I like, but I don't cook and I don't drink. I have no time for your angsty middle-aged bullshit. Grow up. I'm really much nicer than this.

Excitement

Near the end, the husband starts talking about excitement, he wants excitement. He says *I think we're in different phases of life.*

Really, she says. We wish you could see her face here, but you can probably guess that she's not smiling. She's hard not-smiling.

What phase am I in, tell me, is it the shuffleboard phase? He says she takes naps and watches TV all the time (habits in place since the Carter administration, which is to say, also in place when they met) and in terms of the excitement he's looking for mentions mostly the biking and the hiking and the cooking. Not one of these things is exciting to her. They're activities in which she could find degrees of enjoyment, but excitement seems like a stretch. She feels she has actual excitement in her life. She thinks, I have so much more excitement than you, dude. She thinks *dude* in her head about her husband right now. She has a willingness to participate in some of these activities, and hopes that he will have a willingness to meet some of her unmet needs. Excitement is not something she's ever actively sought, though even he has pointed out how surprised he was that she went into the city as often as she did after they moved upstate. Her work life provides her with a great deal of excitement. But too much excitement makes her want to drink. She used to drink when she got too excited. (She also used to drink when she got too sad, there was never a reason not to drink, but extremes of feeling on either end were her primary motivations for drinking.) When she gets excited she stays awake all night after she gets home, replaying all the excitement, and is glad that the excitement happened and then is glad that she can watch TV and be plain-old content for a while.

I think I have plenty of excitement in my life, she says. Maybe he lacks excitement in his own work life? She knows that window restoration is meaningful to him, and even satisfying. She also knows that he's not making art lately and he hasn't read her most recent book and there might be a road between those two things. It takes her some time to figure out that as much as anything else it's sex where he wants the excitement. She's not looking for excitement in sex now. She's not against it. She wants tenderness, familiarity. She's not saying she doesn't want hot sex. They try a few new things. Trust us when we tell you it's nothing you'd have to google. The husband expresses gratitude for the wife's openness and his satisfaction appears obvious. But really, she knows he has an idea now that it will only ever be exciting again with someone else.

California Screamin'

The wife and the husband have been separated for three weeks. This week the wife is at work in California. She has had this job for almost ten years, the longest she's had any job. The wife loves the work, loves the ten days she spends there every six months. These ten days are a little different. She's grateful to be among friends and working, a purposeful distraction. But there are no nightly check-ins with the husband this time. She talks to him only once or twice while she's away, both times about the dog. There are no *I miss you* texts, no nothing. They have barely spoken over the last three weeks. Prior to this, they've never had so much as a fight where they stopped speaking for an hour. She maybe left the room to take a few deep breaths one time. Late afternoon or after dinner, she thinks, This is when I'd be calling him.

The wife looks at their checking balance to make sure there's enough for a withdrawal and finds a bank charge that indicates he's taken the client to the movies. She knows the husband and the client are exploring. There have been no previous such expenditures, and it's only thirty bucks, but her response is as epic as though she has just discovered an affair, as though she has just discovered the piles of receipts for hotel rooms and weekends away and lingerie and jewels that weren't given to her. She picks up the phone.

Did you take her to the movies?

Yeah.

We don't have a budget for dating.

Oh. I guess I hadn't thought about that. Sorry.

Please don't do it again. Go Dutch or let her fucking pay. She's got money.

They hang up and she has a good sob, pulls herself together to show up for a faculty party. It's right downstairs. She wants to skip it, but there's a colleague she loves who she doesn't get to see often. She doesn't want to cry at the party. But she should eat. She sits down with some of her work buddies, relays what has just happened. Heads shake. Her friends make her laugh while she's crying into her pasta. A party guest asks if she can take the empty seat at the table across from them. *Of course,* she says.

There's no use pretending she hasn't been crying. *Hi we met at breakfast this morning, my husband and I just separated!*

Been there, the party guest says.

Fuck Marry Kill

She is marry. In this game you stick to your picks, in this order. You get the fuck out of your system, you marry the best one, you kill the worst one, game over. When she was twenty-one or twenty-five and you and she were drunk you and she both might have thought she was fuck but she was always and would only ever be marry. She would have been marry even if she'd never married. This game is not called Fuck Marry Kill Divorce.

Philadelphia

The husband and wife have couples therapy scheduled for the day after her return. It's a dodgy plan at best because there are so often travel delays to and from California to their place in upstate New York. There are never less than two connections, it's an especially long travel day on the way east, and she's always tired from ten days of work. The husband will not be meeting her at the airport, the husband will not be sending her loving texts telling her to breathe, that everything will be okay. The husband may as well be sending her texts that say *Nothing is going to be okay ever. I lied. Don't bother breathing.*

A flight delay in Phoenix lands her in Philadelphia long past the last flight home. Sometime after midnight, all passengers with connecting flights are directed to guest relations to pick up hotel vouchers. It's a long walk from their gate to a long line at guest relations. It's twelve thirty. It's one a.m. It's one thirty. *Just breathe, everything will be okay.* It doesn't work as well when you try to tell yourself. *There are no more hotel vouchers, I'm terribly sorry for the inconvenience.* There are also no rooms at no hotels in no city near Philly. *There's one in some suburb thirty miles away, do you want that?* The wife knows how that will go. It will maybe get her a nap in a bed before she has to turn around and come back to the airport and unpack and repack and go through security again and and and no she does not want that. She wants this airline to make her husband get his shit together, call him on the phone right now and wake him up and tell him he fucked up and to just get his shit together. She grabs onto the counter so she will not fall on the floor from the breakdown that is about to happen. *Here's a fifteen-dollar voucher for food anywhere in the airport. If you go to information at Gate Whatever they will get you a cot and a blanket.*

Where is that? Is it on the other side of the airport? It's one a.m. I've been traveling all day, I've been traveling through this goddamned airport to get to this desk for a hotel voucher, I cannot travel beyond this counter so far as that chair behind me, just give me a pillow for my head, I'll put it right here on the counter. My husband is leaving me. She maybe doesn't say that last thing.

A guy in one of those carts pulls up.

Here, this guy will give you a ride to the info desk.

I'm sorry, she says to the cart guy, unable to stop crying. Cart guy shrugs. Cart guy doesn't care. Cart guy works in an airport. Cart guy has seen this. Cart guy sees this every day.

There is no one at the info desk. That there is no one at the info desk is epically disastrous. Whatever life skills she's banked have been spent on this one travel day. She has been flying alone since she was nine years old and she is tired now. If she ever gets home, she will stay home, and never set foot in an airport again. Info desk guy comes. *There are no more cots right now. Maybe later.* It is already later. It cannot be later than it is. It is the latest it will ever be. The wife sees some red club chairs by a window. It should be noted that the Philadelphia airport, if you happen to have a layover during normal hours, when you are not slowly losing your shit, has many enjoyable places to sit, charge your phone, even download a book for free. The club chairs are the closest chairs and that is where she will sleep. That the club chairs are on something of a ramp, and therefore slanted, at this point, is irrelevant. She has no remaining energy to go in search of a level floor. She'll put her head on the high end. She'll put a coffee table between the two club chairs and stretch out and use her purse as a pillow. Info guy walks by her setup twenty minutes later to report that there are cots now over by the info desk. She cannot walk back there now. It is maybe twenty feet away. Info guy brings her a pillow and a blanket. There is also holiday Muzak. It's two a.m. and her marriage is falling apart and she's on a bed made of two club chairs and a coffee table slanting downhill at the Philadelphia airport. She phones a friend who communicates largely in metaphors. *This is totally his fault,* the wife says. Metaphor friend doesn't ask how so, knows that her friend is in a bad place. *I let myself believe he meant it when he said he'd never leave.* Metaphor friend offers to stay on the phone until she falls asleep if she needs to. Metaphor friend tries out a few metaphors (slow kiddie trains at the mall, slow cookers, broken arms healing, anything that's generally slow), somehow makes her laugh, talks to her until she's calm enough to sleep for maybe an hour.

The wife plugs in her headphones, puts some TV show on her iPad to drown out her brain, and closes her eyes. But there will be no sleep, only a tornado of thoughts about the imminent and complete demise of her marriage.

You Go

At home she showers the airport off her and asks the husband if she can ride to therapy with him. She planned to meet him there but it's a half-hour drive and we've already discussed her driving issues when she's not tired and about to end her marriage. He says he doesn't think it's a good idea. She says *We don't have to talk. I just can't drive.* They ride there together mostly in silence.

I don't really know what to say now, the wife says in therapy. *You go.*

He says he knows she wanted him to take his time, not make a rush decision. But he's spent a lot of time thinking about this these last three weeks. He's very sure, having thought about it for three weeks, that he wants to end the marriage. *We had a good marriage, I'm not willing to work on it, I chose someone else.*

They ride home together mostly in silence. At the end of a marriage, do you hug goodbye? She can barely squeak out the word.

New Love Story

She tells her husband a story about young love. How when you're young, like teenage young, and you meet a boy and you maybe don't even have anything to talk about but he's the absolute cutest or maybe you have everything to talk about but either way his hair is shaggy perfection, the kind that his mom thinks is well ready for a haircut but she's wrong, and you're at the beach, this boy's hair is only made more glorious by sun and sand and salt, and you're at your best friend's family's beach house for the summer and you and your best friend and some of the other kids are hanging out, or maybe around, on a stoop outside the ice cream place, and then people break off, your friend has a new boyfriend, sort of, and you and the boy walk home via the beach, or he rides you home on the handlebars of his bike, the ride is wobbly in that way that's both scary and fun, and it's dark now, and it doesn't even matter what happens next, you're on the handlebars of a cute boy's bike in the dark, leaning back the tiniest bit into his shoulders, and when you hop off by your best friend's house, you maybe kiss or you maybe don't, you probably don't, but the thing about it that makes it what it is, that you don't know right now, is the newness of it. You're a teenager, you think you've seen things already, you're not a baby, you're no baby seeing a puppy or an airplane for the first time, except you are, and you maybe kiss or you maybe don't, but you will feel something in your body either way, you will feel something, maybe everything, with the totality of your body, and the thing is, there is a lot you don't know right now, you don't know if he likes you likes you, you don't know if you'll see him after the summer because he lives somewhere in Westchester, which is a whole train ride away and who ever goes there, what even is Westchester, maybe he will write you letters from Westchester, and you hop off his handlebars and run upstairs to your best friend's room to tell her all about it, and to discuss what it meant or might mean or could mean, and what it felt like when your shoulder touched his shoulder, like you have no words, even, and you ask her, again, what is it like to kiss a boy, because you don't know, you haven't actually kissed anyone yet, maybe kissing will be terrible and disgusting, probably not, but maybe, because remember those kissing parties where we stood by the onion dip, no way were we going to get involved in that, it really did look disgusting, like you didn't have to have any clue how to do it to know that they for sure had no clue how to do it, plus you'd just seen half of them eating a bunch of onion dip, and she says *That was so gross!* and she tells you all about what it's really like, that it's totally not gross, that with the right boy you will never want to stop kissing, and then you will want to do other things, and you scream and she screams and you fall over laughing, but you want to know when it will happen, when will it happen, will it happen, how can you make it happen, what is the exact right outfit and what is the exact right next move to assure that you will be kissed, you will lie awake for hours on this night imagining and planning and feeling these things in your body that you might not even be made to feel by the cute boy, you don't know, but above all else, above all else of what you don't know, you don't know how few times in your life you might have any exciting bit of this, because even if you spend the rest of your life with cute hair boy like you're dreaming about right now, the one thing it won't be when you're having your golden wedding anniversary is new. She tells her husband this story and she says *But what you get is something else, something deeper, something richer, history, intimacy*, like maybe she's trying to convince herself, even, and he nods, and then two months later, when they're in couples counseling for what will be the last time, and he says he wants to end the marriage, and he says that thing, *We had a good marriage, I'm not willing to work on it, I chose someone else*, the next (and last) thing he says is *I want new love.*

The Story Will Not Be the Whole Story

You don't know the half of it. Maybe I don't know the half of it. I don't think I do know the half of it.

Catastrophe

She has seen every episode of *Fixer Upper* at least three or four times. She has seen every episode of *Property Brothers* as many times. She has seen people hunt for houses in this country and she has seen them hunt for houses internationally. She has studied all the home improvement shows for ideas for her own home. She can't watch any of them now. She can't watch any movie she saw with her husband. She definitely can't go see that show at the Met Breuer that she's interested in, and forget about art fairs ever. She can't listen to any music she listened to with her husband. Please never speak the name of Robert Pollard within a one-mile radius around her. She can barely listen to some of the music she listened to while she was with her husband that he never listened to at all. She can't watch any show that she and her husband watched together, which is fairly disappointing with regard to shows that are still on. Because if she does any of these things she will think about him, and the marriage, and she will think of things she might want to say to him about these things and she doesn't want to think about him or the marriage for any more moments of the day than she already does, which is marriage-thinking-heavy as it is. She doesn't want to say anything to him about anything now. Actually that's not true. She wants to say many things to him and she wants him to say things back that will make any of this make sense, but it has so far been established that whenever any sense is made, soon enough it will be made even more senseless than it was in the first place, and so she's more or less trying whatever she can to prevent herself from saying things in the hope that at some point she will actually stop wanting to say things. Please don't tell her how good *Catastrophe* is this season. She doesn't want to know.

So Much

So smart so talented so so so foxy so easy so fun so kind so good to him he loved her so much so so much he was the luckiest she chose me she drank the wrong kind of coffee ate the wrong kind of cookies didn't eat the way he thought she should eat in general didn't cook like his mom cooked didn't cook at all didn't like spicy food didn't know what good food was didn't make the bed the right way spent too much money on magazines newspapers books could be more affectionate could be more seductive could watch less TV could stay up later could be more this could be more that could be more could be more could be more

Shirts

What do you think of this, he asks her. The husband shows the wife four shirts the new client has gotten him as a thank-you gift. The wife estimates that these are $100 shirts, maybe 125, maybe 150. Nice shirts. Shirts they don't have the budget for, or not four at a time, anyway. The wife never buys any shirts besides t-shirts for the husband. She's been shirt shopping with him. *This hem isn't right. That color is weird. Those sleeves are too short. This cut doesn't look good on me.*

I think it's too much, the wife says.

Yeah, me too, says the husband. He's asking what she thinks, though, and she leaves out the part about thinking that this woman is interested in her husband.

Dresses

The client has a studio sale, dresses from past collections she hasn't sold. She used to be a designer. Jersey dresses, lots of volume here, fit there. The kind that you can't always make sense of on the hanger but that look way better once you get them on. The husband and wife go together. The wife tries on a few. She lands on one. Ginger Rogers in a nautical-themed movie, navy fitted bodice, three-quarter sleeves, ankle-length navy-and-white-striped voluminous skirt. It looks great on her, but it's a mood. She's not a long-dress person. She asks the client how much. The client smiles coyly and whispers in her ear. *It's free.* The wife isn't sure she hears the client right, asks her to say it again, again the client whispers *It's free,* and we need to add here that it's a sexy whisper, like the client is meaning to seduce the wife as well as the husband, or at least put her under a spell. The wife says *No, no, I have to give you something.* She lets the wife give her seventy-five dollars. The dress does not get worn. The husband and wife separate so that he can explore with the client. There has been no time for there to be a mood for the dress. Now there's a new mood. The mood is burn the fucking dress. But she doesn't want to burn her house down with it, so the dress goes out with the trash. She puts it on top of the bin, puts it back in the bin. She has a fantasy that someone will pull it out of the trash, wear it around town.

Unlikely

She wanted to paint her office and the closet. He said it had to be done a certain way. She waited for him to do it. He had other things to do on the house, he worked, there was only so much time, he moved out. She will paint the office and the closet. She will patch and sand and paint. She chooses, impulsively, unlikely colors even for her, a Tiffany Blue for the closet, a bright orangey yellow for the office. Colors that would surely not be approved. She paints the office and the closet, gets paint on the trim, on the ceiling. It would be cool if that were on purpose even a little but it isn't. It basically looks fine. And he doesn't live there now. But he will see it. He will see it and he will hate it. He emails to schedule a time to pick up some clothes when she's not there, and after he leaves he emails again to say he really likes the paint colors she chose.

Well This Is Interesting

On a trip to the city, a friend takes her to dinner. It's not a date, she's not ready for a date, what is that even. It feels like one of the best dates she's ever had, but they're just friends, okay yes, they're friends who did it a couple times a million years ago but still it's not a date. Even though he tells her like sixteen times that she looks fucking amazing and sexy as shit and holds her hand and asks her a million questions and listens to what she's saying and looks in her eyes while they're talking and orders oysters and appetizers and pays for dinner and they walk across the village for dessert. Not a date.

But it feels like a date, and it especially feels like a date in her pants, and it's when she has this feeling in her pants that she thinks to herself, Well this is interesting, because she and her husband have been collaborating (well look at that) on this whole story that it takes her way longer to get going, and here she is getting going, and she's in a restaurant basically just having a conversation. It isn't until later that she stops to think more about it, not about what might happen with her friend, but about what hasn't happened with the husband for a good little while, something she's been telling herself is about her, and her body, and is maybe not about her or her body, or at least not in the draft of the story they co-wrote about it, and has been about not engaging with her husband in this way for a good little while.

Fire Island

She's been going to Fire Island since she was about twelve or thirteen, with her lifelong best friend, whose family has a house there. She spent enough time there growing up to become part of a crew of kids she's known ever since. In college she spent a whole summer there working as a cocktail waitress. She has made out with boys on the beach. She has forgotten them over the winter and made out with their brothers the next summer. She has made out with boys her friends have made out with in previous summers and compared notes. She has been called a Fire Islander by Fire Islanders, about which she has a weird kind of pride. She has, for the most part, nothing but great memories associated with Fire Island, which is something she can't say about any other place in the world.

This time she's here for two weeks, basically by herself, basically on vacation, although she's not sure what that means exactly. Her best friend's house is not entirely preserved in amber, but the vibe is still very much *We bought this house in the sixties with the furniture still in it.* She likes things that don't change. In theory, she likes things that change too, but when there's a change that you do not plan, a major change that is decided for you, when you know you can come out to a place where you grew up and find it like it was forty years ago, it's a bit easier to access that hope you had for the future when you were twelve and sixteen and twenty-one.

She meets a friend from her old crew for a morning walk on the beach. The only thing that's notably different about it now is that they text to meet up. You used to just meet up. You knew you'd see each other on the beach, or in town (= a few blocks over where the candy store and pinball room are), or people would just stop by. You might have picked up the phone a time or two. But they aren't teenagers now, and they aren't here forever now. Go ahead and assume that these two made out on the beach in 1980 or something, whether they did or not. They did, though. But they were only ever friends. Occasionally there was a more fully realized boyfriend-girlfriend situation in their loose crew, but mostly it was exactly what summer romance had to be, by definition.

So they walk on the beach and they catch up on the last ten years or so since they've seen each other and she's pretty sure she's being flirted with, knowing this person and this place and its history and their history, though current circumstances make flirting, well, weird. She's not interested in flirting and hardly remembers how anyway, although she's not completely opposed to being flirted with. But she's still married, and she's been married for a long time. She may not be married for much longer, but she's married now, and she's been separated for about five minutes. She still has no idea what happened in her marriage, not really. Her husband moved out just over a month ago.

She came here to get away, get a different view, cry in a new location. Maybe crying with a view of the ocean would be better than crying on her sofa. She knew she might be risking her romantic view of Fire Island as the magical place where boys noticed her for the first time, where her day was made up of bike rides and beach glass and no cars and cans of Tab and her best friend, that if she chose this place for this purpose, one possible outcome would be that forevermore her Fire Island romance would be bittersweet at best and totally ruined at worst. But yesterday was made up of bike rides and beach glass and no cars and giggling with her best friend like they were still fourteen, and yes, crying, and today she's walking on the beach with a cute fifty-seven-year-old boy who still thinks she's cute. *Who would leave you?* he says.

This is what I keep asking myself, she says.

Vermont

So now friends are inviting her places, so many places, mostly where they live, next up, Vermont. Vermont is not far. She could drive to Vermont, maybe. It's possible. No major cities to pass through, no major traffic hassles. Her friends in Vermont stay at their family's *camp* on a lake. That's what they call it. She doesn't know anyone who lives at a camp, doesn't have a vision for this camp until she gets there and sees that there's nothing else you could call it. A bunch of rustic cabins and a bunkhouse on a property on a lake with inner tubes and kayaks.

Kayaks! A *Dateline* episode airs not long before her Vermont trip, about a couple who went out kayaking on the river about two miles from her house. Only one of them returned. She had little interest in kayaking before this news broke, zero after. She does not need a real-life *Dateline* of her own, where she floats down the Hudson never to return. Growing up, she used to go canoeing on her grandparents' pond. That pond was not a small pond, but it was by definition a pond: maybe six feet deep in the very middle, a pond you could for sure swim across in a couple minutes if you had to. These are her preferred boating conditions.

The husband wants to hike, the husband wants excitement, the husband leaves. The wife will drive to Vermont and the wife will go kayaking, on a lake she can't swim across, and she will enjoy it very much. It feels like a big fucking deal until it doesn't. It feels a little bit exciting.

Tuscany

Another friend runs women's retreats in different locations around the country and around the world. The wife is driving around town crying as usual and her retreat friend calls and says *You need to come on this trip, it will change your life*, and she's thinking she's had about enough life change for one year. She doesn't honestly think anything is going to get her from sad to not sad at this point. She knows being in Italy with her friend would not suck. But this trip is less than a month away, and she begins to list all the reasons she can't go, starting and ending with no money, and retreat friend is like *We can work it out*, and she's like *I don't have it*, and retreat friend is like *Could you get airfare*, and she's like *I'd still have to pay for a dog-sitter, the husband is being weird about dog-sitting now*, and retreat friend is like *Just ask him and call me back*, and so she asks him and he says *Sure no problem* and she calls retreat friend back and says *I guess I'm coming to Italy.* This person is giving her a very big gift. It's overwhelming. It's income her friend could be earning to give away this slot. But it's what she does. Retreat friend is all about giving, listening, making space for people, and connecting them.

On her first night in Italy, at an eight-hundred-year-old stone villa in a field of lavender in Tuscany, retreat friend hands out delicate silver bracelets to each of the women that say *I got you.* They all put them on and they all leave them on.

There are twenty-five women at this retreat, five who are here on a scholarship. Retreat friend raises money for women to come who have recently suffered some type of serious loss. Loss here meaning death of a close loved one, not meaning their husband had a midlife crisis and left. It is not a grief retreat, but once they all start meditating, doing yoga, writing exercises, grief emerges as an overarching theme. The wife understands that she's grieving the marriage, and she knows other kinds of loss too. But she hasn't lost a partner, or a child, or both. So she feels a bit self-conscious about being raw in the way that she is, among these women. For about five minutes. These women, funny, joyful, and heartbroken, fully understand that grief isn't one thing. These women are present in their lives and their feelings. These women share their stories with the wife and when the wife shares her story they tell her about their own divorces. They know. *You're grieving, this is normal.*

By the end of the week the wife is in love with twenty-five women and a border collie covered in burrs. She's still in her grief when she leaves. She's still in her grief now. She doesn't go from sad to not sad. She just goes.

Pilot

From there she lands in the city, back in the fancy couple's East Village pied-à-terre. As you know, in a sitcom, this sweet, improbably large apartment, soon to be nicknamed The Mansion by the teenage members of the cast, would never be explained, but this is real life. It's an apartment this fifty-something creative writing professor could never afford, but in this show, it gets explained and things begin to turn around, at least to the extent that it offers her an extended break in which she won't run into her husband, and that she can see friends every day, and go to meetings every day all day if she wants. She brings one suitcase and her laptop and the dog, and this is where the sitcommy turn of events takes place: her old buddy the single dad, the one from the Woodstock trip, along with his teenage daughter, moves back to the city after twenty years in LA, buddy needs a place to crash for a week or two while apartment hunting, stays with new divorcée-to-be, never leaves, says it's no coincidence that they ended up in New York at the same time, divorcée-to-be stares directly into the camera, divorcée-to-be cries on single dad's shoulder, single dad holds her hand and makes her laugh, teenage daughter and her friends burst through the door without keys, quirky makeshift family and comedy ensue.

This Kid

The first time she meets the kid, on a walk through Central Park with her old bud, the kid shares a personal story and she's funny and real and she cries so the wife gives the kid a tissue and tells her she's awesome but holds back an impulse to tell her that she loves her. She doesn't want to freak the kid out, this kid doesn't really know her, this is her dad's old friend she met one time when the kid was twelve. She's eighteen now, casually cool, all big sweatshirts and sneakers and high-waisted jeans and scrunchies, which are back, and she can lip-synch to a Drake song like nobody's business; in the summers she goes to some outdoorsy camp and mentors young girls and goes on ice climbing/canoeing/we don't even know what kind of expeditions in Alaska and Michigan and places, plus she *writes*, and wants to do sixteen other things with her life and we're pretty sure the ice-climbing kid can accomplish whatever the hell else she wants. At this point the wife can barely navigate a sidewalk free of ice without risk of breaking a bone, and when they say goodbye, the kid hugs her and says *I love you* and she says *I love you too*, and then she feels like a dope, an elated dope, for not having said it first.

Different

Liquid hand soap.

One of those diffusers that plugs into the wall.

Air freshener, sometimes.

Something called Kaboom.

Tide.

Dish towels laid out on the counter.

Paper plates, sometimes. The apartment has a dishwasher. She wonders about this too until her old bud explains that there were always lots of kids at his house and he'd have endless dishes piled up if he didn't. Now there are always lots of kids at their house.

Not one of these things matters to her. They're housemates anyway, not a couple, but he's a dude and she's living with him. These things are just different things. All the things are different.

Whatever We Are

Leaving one of their neighborhood joints, she and her old buddy get caught in the rain. She's brought an umbrella but he declines her offer to share.

No! he says. *I am going to embrace this experience! I am loving this experience!*

He is very clearly not loving this experience, as the rain is pelting him directly in the face, but he is laughing about it.

I'm Ryan Gosling in The Notebook, *if they had a scene somewhere in between Gosling and Garner!*

When they stop at a crosswalk, she kisses him on the cheek.

Regularly, she finds herself trying to explain her relationship with her old friend. People ask. *We're just friends,* she'll say. But it's something more than *just,* something other than *just. We're very close,* she'll say. *We're whatever we are,* she'll say. *We're Bert and Ernie.*

We're housebuds.

Fun

Her old bud texts on his way home to say he canceled his dinner plans. *Wanna maybe watch something?*

Sure.

What kind of food are you in the mood for?

Pizza!

He returns with a pizza while she's cutting and pasting an outline for a project.

WHOA what is going on, am I interrupting your ransom letter?

This is what revisions look like sometimes.

Hey were you having bad dreams all night?

Oh god. Probably. I remember talking to someone.

This was not talking, this was an FBI interrogation. Someone did something very wrong. You were screaming like a gargoyle was inside you. I was afraid to come in and check, like some creature would emerge and swallow me.

I do have a history of bad dreams. And screaming in my sleep.

They settle into the sofa. She's so comfortable with her old buddy; they've known each other for twenty-seven years. Can comfort be trusted anymore? She knew her husband for sixteen. She always felt comfortable with him too. Is this what he meant by wanting excitement, that they were too comfortable with each other? Who is interested in discomfort? Not her.

Can I ask you something? he says.

Of course.

This is all so easy with us, like, I just can't believe how easy. You're so easy! Were you this same way with your husband? She knows he knows the answer to this, that he's mostly making a point.

I was exactly like this!

There's something wrong with him, he says. *You're so easy to be with. You're never annoying.*

She is not a compliment hound, generally, but needs more than *not annoying.* She gives him a beat to figure that out.

I mean, you're more than not annoying! You know that!

Am I fun?

How much do we laugh every night?

So much.

You're so fun. Her bud is many things, nothing if not a shit ton of fun. *You know I don't toss out "fun" easily. I have a high standard for fun. You're so fun.*

Yeah, I think I'm fun too.

Mild

Sometimes they go grocery shopping together. Maybe that's what house-mates do. She hasn't had a housemate since 1993. It feels a lot like when she shopped with her husband. When they first started dating they'd drive all the way to the North Side of Chicago to Trader Joe's, get stuff to make dinner together. There was always lots of hugging up and down the aisles. There was hugging in Trader Joe's until the end. Maybe there was something to see there, that shopping for food together had always meant something to him, the idea that they would make meals together. They did make some meals together now and again. Would have been nice if they had always kept making meals together, why didn't they always make meals together? At some point there were fewer meals made together. She should probably blame herself for that. Not for not cooking. Just for letting that go. Yes. She should surely blame herself for that.

There's hugging in Westside Market too, different guy, her old bud, but now with more questions because they don't know what everyone likes or doesn't like, and more meal planning because one of them is actually going to cook, then more hugging. Is hugging in grocery stores a thing? This is a question, not a complaint.

Should we get some chicken cutlets?

Let's do.

Do you like spicy spaghetti sauce or mild?

Mild. Always mild, she says. She waits for a judgment that doesn't come.

Okay, mild. What kind of cheese do you like for grilled cheese?

Any kind of cheese.

I like mild cheddar.

Then we get mild cheddar, she says.

What about soup, should we have some soup with it?

I love soup and grilled cheese.

How about tomato basil?

Yes, tomato basil.

He pulls some pancake mix off the shelf.

Would you eat pancakes?

If you make them? Um, yeah.

Okay then we also have to get some real maple syrup.

I think you're my platonic life partner now, she says.

PLP! he says. *You're down with PLP?*

Yeah you know me, she says.

Remember onion dip?

Sure, do you want me to make some onion dip?

You know how to make onion dip?

Um, everyone knows how to make onion dip?

I don't know how to make onion dip!

Okay, I'll make onion dip.

Are you sure it's not too much trouble?

It's two things that you put together, she says, *and we already have one of them at home.*

If you're sure, wow, that would be so great!

They're in the store for a while. She always goes with a list. She is learning that her bud likes to consider all options on the fly. She is learning that he will stand in front of the ice cream freezer alone for ten minutes, considering mood and discussing nuances of flavors, which can be very entertaining, but she is also learning that there is a point at which he needs a gentle nudge toward the door.

At home she starts to show him how to make onion dip for when they're not living together anymore. *I don't want to think about that right now,* he says.

> *Onion dip, or us not living together anymore?*

> *Both,* he says, digging into the chips and dip. *Man, whoever doesn't know what a great catch you are is a fool.*

> *Because I make onion dip?*

> *Yes, because you make onion dip.*

> And once again she doesn't understand anything.

She may have taken this mundane grocery store scene past the point she's trying to make with it, which is both that it is mundane, and that she's doing it with someone who isn't her husband.

Party

They've been roommates for about a month now. The old bud has re-
trieved some of his things from storage: a mirror for above the fireplace
mantel, pillows and throws, dining room chairs, large colorful abstracts
painted by a friend. The wife and her bud spend some time moving the
paintings around to find their right places. It's not a huge makeover, but
this apartment lacked for art and anything more than bare-bones furniture, and it now looks like a place where people actually live. Her movie
has been going around the festival circuit this year and is about to be
screened again, this time at a small festival in the city.

*What do you think about the idea of having a few people over before
the screening?* she asks. *A few of our friends, a few people from the cast and
crew.*

I think it's a great idea.

He spends the afternoon vacuuming and cleaning the high windows
in the living room that are nearly black with soot from the bus stop in
front of the building. They get another good music mix going. There is
more singing and dancing.

The kid comes over early to do the wife's makeup. The kid is way into
makeup. The kid is into ice climbing and writing and makeup. The kid
sets the wife up on a barstool in the kitchen, where there's the most light.

She takes her time. The wife looks in the mirror. One more thing the kid is good at. It's pretty and subtle, way more subtle than the wife expects it to be even though it takes her some time. The wife doesn't realize until she sees the photos later how good it looks. Her friends and family show up for the party. It goes well. *That went well!* her bud says. They take the party over to the screening. The response to the movie is good. Again. There's an awards ceremony afterward. It's a tiny indie festival, she didn't even realize there were awards. The director of the tiny indie festival comes out after the screening to hand out the awards. He says the title of their movie. He hands the award to the director and to her. Their movie wins best feature. *Best feature. Red carpet photos.* These are words she says in sentences this year.

Sometime around midnight, the wife, her bud, the kid, and her boyfriend head to a diner. It has those giant phone book–sized menus, with glossy photos of menu options. They're all a little punchy because it's been a big day and they're hungry. Housebud points to something on the menu when the waiter comes. Something about this is hilarious to the wife and the kid, though it cannot be explained, and they nearly slide under the table laughing until their stomachs hurt. The kid's boyfriend and her bud look at each other, wondering what's so funny. *I dunno,* her bud says, *but I'm pretty sure it was at my expense.*

Widow

So this is one of those things about the age difference: it seems like a given that the older one will die first. That's the logical order of things. But death is no place for logic. The husband's parents both died young, at thirty-five and fifty-one, the wife's mom died at sixty-three. The couple knew that either one of them could go first. In the beginning, she hoped that he'd go first, not because she wanted that, but because she didn't want him to have any more loss in his life. (Plus she sort of thought she'd do better on her own, or that he might choose a horrible person, quickly, like her stepdad did. Her stepdad's brand-new and horrible girlfriend moved into her mom's house four months after she died. *Oh yeah,* they all said, *that's a real thing. It happened to my* _____ [fill in relative here].) She made the punk friends promise that if she went first, they wouldn't let him have a horrible girlfriend; she hoped he would have one, but only if she were awesome and great. She had not thought about the need for horrible-girlfriend prevention under any other circumstances.

Every two weeks, the wife makes the commute home for couples therapy (round two, post-game). Today they're sitting on a small grassy hill in the parking lot, talking about the tornado that touched down in their city in May, the day before he moved out. *I knew when the tornado hit,* he says.

The client's car was crushed under a tree. The client wasn't in it at the time, but the husband admitted that he was hit hard to think of what might have happened to her.

What about what might have happened to me, she says. *I was alone in the basement with the dog.*

He makes a facial version of a shrug.

Is this the moment to call it and walk away? It's already been called anyway. They've been making bits of progress in terms of trying to understand one another. At least he's being honest?

This is really terrible, he says, *but I've thought about you being dead.* She takes this in for about a second, isn't in the mood to take the attendant feelings all the way.

Well, that is normal, I've thought about that too. Fuck you.

You have? He brightens up and then she's sorry she said it, like she's let him off the hook, or at least is trying to indicate it's not the end of the world, when she also means to hurt him a little bit.

Don't you remember This Is 40? *They talk about their fantasies about murdering the other person.*

That wasn't a very good movie though.

Whatever. It was there because it's common.

What she doesn't tell him: how many times she wished he'd die first so there was no chance they'd ever get divorced. How many times she constructed a fantasy about someone else that began with her being a widow, because she didn't want to imagine them divorced. Constructing a fantasy about someone else never includes the option of an open marriage. Her best sexual fantasies always involve romance and intimacy, and she knows she can't compartmentalize that. Monogamy, even in her fantasy life.

While We're Here: Ten Scenarios That Might Have Been Preferable

(for Dad, who kept a list of the top ten ways
he was going to die)

1. The wife is stricken with a terrible, fatal illness while they're still in couples therapy. He stays with her out of guilt and she's fine with that. Eventually he realizes what a heinous mistake he was about to make and spends the rest of her living days atoning by reading to her, washing her hair, and bearing gifts of fine jewelry.

2. The husband falls from a second-floor window at the client's house while he's still in couples therapy with the wife, who outfits the home with a ramp and one of those chairlifts that runs up the stairs and when he returns home from the hospital she cares for him for the rest of his living days. He realizes how lucky he was to have her all those years and spends the rest of his living days expressing his gratitude.

3. The wife, still conscious on her deathbed after falling down in front of a car years before the horrible client comes into the picture, years before they ever go to couples therapy, tells her husband not to cry, that even though she had a short life, she had everything she ever wanted, and she coughs an operatic cough and dabs her head with a lacy handkerchief and expires.

4. Returning from couples therapy round three, where they've finally made a breakthrough, pledging their renewed love, they both die in a car accident because the husband is tailgating and there's a tailgater behind them and the car in front of them slows down and there's a pileup. The client shows up at the funeral and the wife's friends stop her at the door and say *Yeah, no, bye,* and then everyone says nice things about how much they loved both of them and how right they were for each other even though the husband went on a stupid walkabout.

5. A year after separating, the wife slips into some morbid reflection and writes it down and then one of these grim scenarios actually happens because that's the superpower she's burdened with, and she has to live with it, on earth or in eternity, depending on which way it goes.

6. Decades after separating and never getting divorced, the husband and wife tentatively and tenderly reunite, only to learn that the husband has a horrible and deadly pulmonary disease from years of working around chemicals. *Everything good in my life was because of you,* he says. *I'm glad you know that now,* she says.

7. Decades after separating and never getting divorced, the husband and wife die separately but meet up in eternity. The husband spends a few eternities trying to make amends, and a few eternities after that, the wife finds forgiveness and they spend all the eternities after that together.

8. Decades after separating and never getting divorced, the husband and wife die separately but meet up in eternity, and in eternity there is no language and no form, only blissful, wordless understanding and love of the human condition. There's

no such thing as sorry in eternity, there are no mistakes or regrets in eternity, zero self-loathing or grief; there's only what is, and what is is good and right and perfect, which means there are infinite puppies.

9. The client was never born, no one else was ever born who either of them found attractive during their fifty years of marriage, and they die peacefully in their sleep holding hands.

10. The husband and wife were never born, and no one's heart ever hurt.

Apples

She still slices apples the way her husband did for her when they were first dating, in circular slices. They hold more peanut butter. She's never seen this done by anyone else, and it charms her, this small thing, and she slices apples this way for the next fifteen years. Now, the husband is gone but the apples still get sliced this way. She doesn't think of the husband every time, only occasionally, especially that one time when she slices right into the tip of her ring finger, when she thinks, Maybe I should slice them differently now.

Priorities

Her bud asks whether or not the husband prioritized her. She has no answer. She thinks maybe she didn't prioritize him. She knows she didn't. She put him right beside her.

Pajamas

While she's in the city, her husband goes to their house to pick up some clothes. Like, all of them, leaving only a pair of her dad's old pajama pants that he sometimes used to wear. Home for therapy, she screams *I hate you* in the empty-plus-pajama-pants closet, over and over. It doesn't matter that it was probably not meant to be a rejection, that it was probably meant to say *These were your dad's, you should have them.* It was probably a no-win for him. She probably wouldn't have thought about the pajamas at all if he'd just taken them. She has other things, better things, to remember her dad by. Now, she's forced to remember that her husband is gone and her dad is gone too.

Last Thanksgiving

Their last Thanksgiving together was not their best ever. He wanted to go out. She wanted to stay home, do it herself. *You don't know how to make a turkey,* he said.

I've done it before, she said. She had made a turkey one Thanksgiving, her first year of sobriety, twenty-five years earlier, she made a turkey and her new sober friends came over, and if she could make a decent turkey coming out of the fog of alcoholism she could probably do it again now.

It's too much trouble for just two people, he said.

Three, she said. *Our friend K doesn't have plans, he'll bring something.*

It's too much, it won't come out good, I don't want to cook, he said.

I'm not asking you to cook. I'm saying I will cook. I've done it before. It came out good. Aren't you the one who always wanted me to cook? She said that to herself.

She made a turkey and it came out good, but the meal and the conversation beyond that are forgotten.

This Thanksgiving

All the firsts are supposed to suck. This is known. But they could suck less. Her first birthday couldn't have sucked more. The husband moved out the day before. That was as suck as it gets. She spent her first post-split wedding anniversary (her fourteenth with her husband, because they are still married) with her best friend, who came up from the city to go to lunch and get massages. This year there are a lot of massages. People give gifts to people going through a divorce, she learns, and often these gifts are massages, and it's a good gift.

She spends her first post-split Thanksgiving with her best friend and her family. That goes fine until the husband texts to say *Hope you're having a nice Thanksgiving (tulip emoji)*. She has learned by this time to be fine with crying in front of whoever but they've all just sat down at the table and she doesn't want to be rude, so she stuffs it this time. He's probably alone. No way would he text her on Thanksgiving with a tulip emoji if he was with his girlfriend. They probably broke up. It doesn't make her happy to think that he might be alone. It doesn't make her happy to wonder what the fuck a tulip emoji means. She eats a bunch of turkey and pie. She's with her best friend. This first is done.

The Kid's Boyfriend

The kid comes over and reads her a story about how she met her boyfriend. She knows the story, of course, because she was there when they met. She and her bud and the kid have lunch at one of those unreasonably charming cafés in the West Village, the dad goes to work and she and the kid leave to go to a meeting. The next one nearby is in the East Village, a clubhouse in a tiny basement room, it's not crowded, a dozen people maybe, a kid about the kid's age sitting in the speaker's chair. He gives a talk and it's good. He has a year sober. His dad is sober. He's funny and he's smart.

Outside after the meeting, the sober kid asks *Are you her mom?* Her bud's kid is still inside talking to someone else. She likes this question. It's the first time she's ever been asked this question. *No,* she says, *I'm friends with her dad.* They chat waiting for the kid to come out, the sober kid tells her he lives in Maplewood, they chat about Maplewood, she knows people in Maplewood, he says *There's a great meeting in Maplewood, you guys should come out sometime,* she thinks, Aw that's sweet, kid, I'm not going to a meeting in Maplewood (she is totally going to a meeting in Maplewood), she tells him she's a writer.

Oh cool, he says, *my dad's a writer,* the bud's kid comes outside, she and the sober kid trade numbers. The sober kid walks back toward the apartment with the wife and the kid, this new sober kid is definitely into her sober kid, they get to the gate in front of her apartment, the wife is like *Okay bye nice meeting you (= no way can I let my friend's kid disappear into the East Village with some random kid from a meeting, not on my watch)*, an hour later the sober kid texts her kid and two days later she's on a train to Maplewood and that's pretty much that. She has a boyfriend now.

So the kid reads the wife this story she's written and the wife has just gotten off the phone with the kid's dad who has moments ago said that thing he says a lot about there being no coincidences, and generally whenever someone says this the wife thinks there are only coincidences, but this time she realizes that the kid would have never met the boyfriend at all if they hadn't gone to that random meeting together and she says *Holy shit, it's not just me and you and your dad, it's all four of us*, and the kid is like *YEAH I KNOW.*

Breakup

Shortly after the Thanksgiving of the Tulip Emoji, the husband emails to make amends of a sort. He says he's sorry for some of the things she wants him to be sorry for. In this email he also mentions that his relationship with the client has ended. He suggests that maybe the wife was right, that he should have taken time to be with himself in the first place, that he will do that now. He suggests that if she wants to know more about the breakup, he will tell her. She sends back a snarky *No thank you, I already know what I need to know* in reply. It does not please her that they have broken up. It pleases her some when people email her, unsolicited, people she doesn't even know well, ranting about how awful a person the client is, using words she would never use. The anger her friends and even some acquaintances have for her husband now is an interesting thing. It makes sense. He hurt their friend. She would feel the same way about people who hurt them. She has anger. She's so fucking angry. It's not her favorite of the feelings. It could be of some use, it could even be appropriate, but she tends to have it for a minute and then it gets doused with tears.

So it does not please her to know that her husband and the client have broken up. It would please her if his girlfriend had never gone all out seducing her husband, it would please her for him to see that for what it was, it would please her if *Don't I get a say* could sound as preposterous to him as it does to her, it would please her if this woman had never come to their town, it would please her if his girlfriend had been a sperm and an egg that never met, it would please her if they could travel back in time to before he took that job when he might have been willing to work with her on their marriage. This news, this does not please her.

A few days later she's walking down 14th Street and says, out loud, to no one *That fucker left me and he didn't fucking stay with her for fucking forever?*

Same

She used to think of herself as a morning person. She liked to get everything done in the morning. Eight to twelve. Those were her best and most productive hours. That was her idea. After that, she could still do whatever she had to do, but wouldn't have the same amount of energy or brightness as she did in the morning. This was the story. So she'd meditate, journal, write, work, run errands all before noon.

In the city, she still doesn't sleep much later than she did before, but she stays up later, goes to a morning meeting, sometimes, eats breakfast at one, sometimes, dinner at nine, sometimes, writes whenever during the day, works whenever during the day, runs errands whenever during the day, naps, sometimes, not always, but whenever, could be one p.m. could be six, almost never gets into bed at eight, will go to a reading at the last minute, will go to a late-night movie at the Angelika after her pajamas are already on, eats ice cream late at night. None of this is exciting, exactly. It's different. It's a little bit exciting. Mostly different. Maybe different really is what her husband meant by excitement. She wanted same.

Let's Talk About the Kid Again

This is maybe the best way to tell you who this kid is: big fun, big personality, big ideas, big faith, big big big giant heart. Her dad's kid for sure and her own person for sure. This is a kid who wants to hang around with the wife. Not all the time, just sometimes. Oftentimes. This is a kid who is only a couple years older than a kid the wife might have had with her husband, if that took, if that had not been permanently shelved. Maybe see also here: *I don't think you'd be a good mother*, maybe. Something about this kid is filling a hole she didn't know was empty, except it's not a random kid hole, it's a this-kid hole. This is a kid who calls the wife when she's sad and asks her to come over and she goes over. This is a kid who can cry on her shoulder and who can cause her to bust into giggles like she's not the age she is. This is a kid who knows she's still growing up, and the wife gets to bear witness to her growing up, beautifully and awkwardly and with the grace of willingness to show up and hang in and do the work through the very worst of it, and seeing this kid actively participating in becoming herself feels like witnessing a miracle. At the kid's age the wife was still actively participating in ruining her life. Now she's the age of using phrases like *at her age*, but it seems she's still becoming herself too, which is honestly annoying as fuck. She had been so sure she was herself before her husband left.

This is a kid who sleeps in the fluffy giant-ass king-size bed with the wife when she comes over but somehow winds up not just on the wife's side but actually on the wife, legs and arms on the wife like she's just a lumpy part of the bed. This is a kid with such an epic story that she once shared it with a roomful of people and held that room like it was hers. The wife sat in the front row laughing and crying, and when we say crying we mean something above and beyond misty tears of appreciation, we mean she broke down, and when we say broke down, we don't mean for a minute, we mean repeatedly, we mean gasping for air sobbing, for the duration of the kid's talk. Maybe that's something some shrink would be able to effectively unpack, maybe it's obvious to you hearing about it, maybe it's about the wife wishing she had a kid, maybe it's about her connecting with the kid's experiences, maybe it's because the kid is so clearly sprung from a person she adores, maybe the wife is still fucking grieving the end of her marriage, maybe it's all these sixteen things or none of these sixteen things maybe in the end it's just big love and that's all anyone needs to know about it.

Christmas Present

Christmas is her jam. Christmas has been a reliably good holiday for most of her life. Christmas had been her mom's thing; her mom, who had her troubles throughout the other 364 days of the year, always made an awesome Christmas, handed down her Christmas traditions, and long before the wife was a wife she always got a tree, carried trees by herself from Broadway and 86th to her apartment on 85th and Riverside, carried trees from 72nd and Amsterdam up five flights to her apartment on 73rd and Columbus, shoved trees into the back of her K-car in Chicago and up a flight to her apartment on Oakley and Erie, often had a tree-trimming party or some other celebration with friends, and had eighteen years of trees as a single adult before she got married.

She is determined to have a merry fucking first Christmas single. This first Christmas single will be so fucking merry she will have two, one in New York with friends and one in Iowa with family, and the one in New York will start with the biggest tree. The apartment has extremely high ceilings. She will get a tree that is as close to the ceiling as it can get. She will go back to her house upstate and fetch her ornaments. Her bud is also super into Christmas. The kid confirms that her dad is super into Christmas. He's stoked to get a tree. But he's out of town and his trip is running long and then she's going to be out of town and time is running out. She texts the kid to say *I need to get a tree ASAP, can't wait for your dad.* The kid texts back *No no you have to wait, he'll be really upset.* She texts her bud and says *I need a treeeeee* with four tree emojis and he texts back:

No

Weeeeee need a treeeee

She texts:

Your kid said you'd be mad if I got one before you came home

He texts:

I'm head of the household (wink emoji)

So I pick the treeee

Then the women tell me no

Then we get the tree you like

But I have to go through the big shot process first and then cave in to what everyone else wants.

Her bud takes the red-eye home. They go straight out for coffee and bagels and in search of more ornaments and lights and a stand. They can't find a proper star so they order a star for the top. They go down Second Avenue to look at trees. Her bud pulls out a fluffy one right in front. It's 350 bucks. Their eyes widen. Her bud asks one of the tree guys what they have closer to 150. Frankly they both think 150 is a lot, both of them have been buying trees for half that at Home Depot for the last bunch of years, but this is NYC, and the tree guys have you at their mercy. *They're all freshly cut, within the last two days, in North Carolina,* tree guy says. Tree guy shows them some lesser trees that still look pretty darn good. Tree guy shows them some even taller trees, trees for people with duplex apartments. *Those go for eight hundred and up,* he says.

Okay let's go back and look at those other ones, they say. They settle on one that looks like it will reach pretty close to their ceiling. It's fluffy and symmetrical and it smells like a tree is supposed to smell. *Wait, what's that one,* her bud says, pointing to a slightly taller one right behind it. She gasps, in a good way.

That one's one-ninety, the tree guy says.

C'mon, her bud says. *Can't you do one-fifty? Look how happy she is.* We have a deal, and tree guy throws in free delivery.

The wife makes ornaments. She makes ornaments for her bud and his kids (he in fact has two) and his kid's boyfriend too, embroidered with everyone's names. They decorate, they sing Mariah Carey's Christmas song nine hundred times, they dance, they laugh. They have a holiday party for the rest of their old friends and when her bud tells the story of the tree, it's longer than this version, and much funnier, and one of the $800 trees they looked at becomes a *reverse hybrid blue spruce.* They're in a holiday movie.

The wife goes bananas shopping for the kid and even for the kid's boyfriend. The kid is an eighteen-year-old girl. She wants Jackie's wardrobe from *That '70s Show.* The wife lived *That '70s Show.* She is going to get the kid all the seventies things. She will get the kid's dad something good as well. Christmas morning, or in this universe, Christmas one p.m. after bagels and iced espresso, on the floor under the giant tree with the dad and the kid, seeing the kid open all the seventies things is every bit of the joy she imagined it would be.

She goes to Iowa after this, back to her family's home, and there's laughter and it's good. They go to Walmart because that's what's there to do, and it isn't until she gets to Walmart looking for last-minute stocking stuffers that she becomes sad. She has bought no presents for the husband. It isn't like she'd have even gone to Walmart shopping for her husband, but packages of white men's t-shirts at Walmart jump off the wall and cuff her in the throat.

No Emergency

The husband is still on all her forms as her emergency contact. What *would* happen if something happened to her? A part of her wants him to have to deal with it if she were in the hospital for some reason. They are still married. You don't get off that easily. Fuck you. She's in the hospital. You sit with her and think about what you've done. Good times. The wife is filling out some forms online and gets to the emergency contact. Her bud says she can put him down.

What if I'm far away in an emergency?

Then I call someone who isn't. Or I come. There's no emergency today.

Two Minutes

For several weeks before the husband comes to the apartment to pick up the dog, her bud entertains her with a number of hypothetical scenarios about how it will go when they all interact. In reality this interaction will last all of about two uncomfortable minutes, if that.

I'm not happy with him, her bud says when the buzzer rings. *I don't think I can pretend to be nice.*

    You don't have to. He's going to come and go.

    What would you do if the two of us actually got into a fight, like a real fistfight?

    She thinks about it for two seconds. In the first second she thinks, Oh my god that would be horrible, and in the second second she smiles and at about the exact second that he's going to say a version of the same thing, she says *I mean, I might be turned on a little bit.*

She opens the door and the husband smiles and he's still so cute, not so cute that she can forget what he's done, but so cute, and she's so anxious about it that she kind of checks out and rushes him out. *Here's his leash, here's his glucosamine, see you in three weeks.*

What Happened

What do you tell people when they ask you what happened? What is the truth to you? Are you so sure you know? How are you so sure? How?

I was with a group recently where everyone went around and shared a memory or a moment from their time together, joyful, weird, beautiful moments. It was a love fest. No dry eyes in the room. Then the last person to speak stood up and began by saying *Well, you know, I'm a truth teller, so*, and you knew pretty immediately that this was going to be a bitter, accusatory truth, and I thought, Is this the kind of truth anyone here needs? I wish I were ever as confident as that person was about what the truth was, but even if I were, does that mean the world needs to hear it? I'm not trying to bring half truths. Not that I know what the fucking truth is. I can try to tell you some things that happened, but other people are free to tell you they didn't, or that they happened a different way.

The day you wake up and tell me you have to go explore, I'm pretty sure the first thing that comes out of my mouth is *So, you want to get separated?* Or maybe *So, I guess you're moving out?* It's one of those, maybe both. Your first response is *What? No!* The conversation from there is a process of sorting out our different ideas about what it means within the context of our marriage for you to *explore* with another person. I remain unsure what I ever could have done in our fifteen years to indicate that there would be any other option than separation, but a sentence you say, at some point on this morning, is *I guess for a minute I thought I was going to have a girlfriend and a wife.* After you determine that the menu of options does not include one from column A and one from column B, or at least not with the wife from column E.C., we still have to parse out where this exploring will happen. I have to parse out for you that it won't happen in our house. That's my bitter, accusatory truth.

Subsequent to this, relevant to truth telling, you tell the first shitty couples therapist that I made you move out. I think you also tell this to the second shitty couples therapist. The first time, I say *No, you don't get to tell the story that way. We didn't have an open marriage. If it hadn't been obvious to you all along that if one of us chose to be with someone else, that one would have to move out, I don't know what else to say.* The second time, when you say *She made me move out,* I correct again. *You chose someone else. Moving out was a given.*

But I'm the one telling the story here. These may be the words that were said, but that doesn't mean I didn't imply that you would have to move out. I did imply it. It was, I believe, inherently implied when we took vows. I believe that you had to have known this would be the end result, and that therefore, no one was making anyone do anything. A choice was being made. By you. A girlfriend instead of a wife.

Do you tell them you wanted a girlfriend and a wife? Did you tell that to your family? Did you tell that to your best friend? Did you tell that to this old friend or that old friend or the other old friend, is that why you don't talk to them much now?

The day you tell me you want to end the marriage, you tell shitty couples therapist number one *We had a good marriage, I'm not willing to work on it, I chose someone else.* Is that what you tell people? I still can't wrap my head around it. But maybe it's the simple truth, and I should swap out the pronouns.

Some of my short answers: He had a midlife crisis. He left me for someone else. He grew distant over time. I let things go that I shouldn't have. I'm broken. I don't know.

Ladies' Choice

Maybe it *was* her choice to end the marriage. He said the words, he said *I want to end the marriage*, after she rejected the only other option presented, of trying an open marriage. She did not want an open marriage. She is happy for any people who choose an open marriage. Her choices became no marriage or open marriage. She chose no marriage. Sometimes choices don't include Keanu Reeves and a private island in the Caribbean as a third option. She had two imperfect options here, and chose the one that worked best for her. In some previous version of herself she very well might have settled for an option that didn't work for her. In this one, she didn't.

Literally

Sometimes my heart literally hurts. I'm using that word the right way.

Promise

Several times over the years, married friends of theirs split up because one partner cheated. Each time, the husband and wife shook their heads.

I don't understand how it gets to that point, why people don't try to work things out, she said.

I don't either, he said.

Promise me that if you're ever thinking about cheating you'll tell me before you do it.

I won't cheat.

Just promise.

Okay. I'll tell you.

The husband keeps this promise.

The Color of Now

She has this thing about lifetimes, like how many of them she's had. The borders of the lifetimes are fuzzy, but she has a visual in her head, a timeline of colors, birth through age six (she doesn't remember this lifetime and these colors are not the colors represented in photographs so all we can say about this time is that we don't know what color it is), first grade through fifth, which is a bright white, sixth grade through high school is yellow, college is all primary colors, her twenties are blue, her early thirties in New York are purple, her late thirties in Chicago are like an orange and pink and purple sunset, her early years with her husband in her early forties are a bright grass green, the last ten years are muted shades of teal and taupe. She has long had the feeling that she's just getting started, though she begins to have a feeling of being settled after they buy the house. You can't see the color of now. It might be red. But you can't really see the color you're in until you're in the next color.

When Will I Believe It

a) one year (nope)

b) one year for every five to seven years of marriage

c) $x = y \times \sqrt{} - \text{lhy}$ (less happy years of marriage)

d) when there are papers

e) when the papers are signed

f) when he pulls such an extreme dick move that I'm angry enough to stop caring

g) never

h) other (use space below)

Us

The kid is having a hard time. A really hard time. Like something-has-to-give hard time. Everything looks good on the outside: friends, school, boyfriend, sobriety. New York City, her dream. Her bud and the kid make a plan for a sit-down. Or a lie-down. The bud likes to have these conferences in the big bed. He's not wrong. The big bed in this apartment is the perfect bed. It's that bed that gets it just right for anyone who enters, firm enough to give good support but with a pillow top that somehow makes you feel like you're lying on a hug. It's a hangout bed when the kids come over, it's a watch-a-movie-in-bed bed, it's a bed for a FaceTime call with your best friend. So they convene in the bed. They make some plans. Together. All three of them. All three of us. For a conversation the wife would love to have had one time with her own parents (okay her own mom), to hear them say that she was okay as she was, that it's okay for her to go on her own path, at her own pace, as many times as she needs to hear it to believe it. The wife takes off her Tuscany bracelet, the one that says *I got you*, puts it on the kid. *I don't think you'd be a good mom.* We think maybe he was wrong. This kid has known me for five minutes. Or months, whichever, the point is she has a history that tells her not to trust me, but this kid has me.

Diners

After their meeting one Sunday she goes to the Westside Diner for lunch with her bud and his kid and four of the kid's friends. One of them is maybe twenty-seven, but the rest are all twenty-one or under. They get a big table, it's not round, like the one that was always reserved for them at the old Cosmic in Columbus Circle, back when they were newly sober, but it's in a similar spot in the front corner window and it's hard not to feel that connection. The waiter takes their order and makes a joke about how many kids they have.

I know! And doesn't my wife look good? her bud says, gesturing in her direction. Everyone at the table cracks up. The fact is, she is plenty old enough to be the mother of the twenty-seven-year-old as well as everyone else at the table and maybe even the thirty-eight-year-old at the table behind them, if it had gone a different way when she was in college. Her bud is joking, but when you're thirty years older than almost everyone at the table, you may find yourself contemplating how you got there.

Time.

You got there with time, which passed until you were old enough to be someone's parent whether you actually were or not.

There is much laughter at the table, much of the usual storytelling by her bud, much talk of the old days when they were the young sober kids at a diner. They have old days now. Bush Sr. was president when they met. Alanis and P.M. Dawn were on repeat. And when you're old enough to have old days, and happen to find yourself around people having new days that look like your old days, connecting as you did back then, having the fun you did, holding each other up like you did, though these kids are fully their own, unique set of characters (as you have been, as you are still), you know, you feel the stupid circle of life or whatever, a melancholic mix of how fast it all goes, as well as an infusion of needed energy and youthful enthusiasm.

There's already been too much talk of gifts here, but she and the bud know how far they've come and they also know that not all of them made it. The conversation turns to what happens when you stay sober long enough.

You get married, you have kids, you get divorced, but because you have so many friends, such a strong support system, when you get divorced, people give you gifts!

Laughter.

They really don't, her bud says. *That is very specifically about you.* You *got gifts.*

The wife laughs hard, keeps talking. An elderly woman with a walker slowly approaches the table, says something the wife doesn't hear. The far end of the table busts out laughing.

One of the kids relays what the woman said. *That lady with the glasses is the loudest!*

Her jaw drops for a second before she laughs; it's not only hilariously rude, but the only other person who ever thought she was even occasionally too loud in public was her husband, who, in her opinion, needed to relax about that.

No no no, but it was like this, her bud says, *she's like, creeping by with her walker with this whole pitiful old-lady act, and then slows her roll even more to drop her bomb: That lady with the glasses is the loudest! But then once she makes her pronouncement, suddenly she speeds out the door like she's on roller skates!*

Another one of the kids, a rapper, says *She heard you say the word "divorce" and she was like "Yo, you think you know what divorce is? I've been divorced five times! Divorce gifts. Get back to me four marriages from now. Pfff." That lady was mad jealous that you were only divorced once.*

The entire table starts riffing on the battle of divorces between the wife and the old lady. They are now all laughing very loudly like their gang did back when they were young in a diner. The wife is not the loudest, not if her bud is at the table, anyway. She wasn't loud at all back in their day, at their table. Their friends were, every one of them, larger-than-life personalities. You had to be loud to be heard in that group, and she used to sometimes wonder how she landed among them. She knew how much she loved them, and how much they loved her. She was never a mouse, she just sometimes felt like she was different. She knows now that she wasn't.

Dog Park

She really does not know why she's crying at the dog park right now. Does there have to be a reason anymore?

Before We're Golden

Nothing has happened. Not one thing has happened at all. I see him rarely now, basically only when he takes the dog, which isn't often since I came to the city. And when I do I feel like I'm talking to a ghost. His body is there, he smiles, he pets the dog, he picks up the dog's leash, and I can see that the leash goes from the dog's body to the body of my husband. It's not floating in midair like you might see in a movie about a ghost ex-husband who comes to walk the dog. *Maybe we should start mediation in June,* I say, *after school ends, it will be a year then*, eliciting only a blank look, the tiniest of nods that could mean yes could mean no could mean could mean could mean, it's kind of a sideways nod, a shrug that's barely even a shrug. I feel like I could wave my arm in front of me and it would go right through him.

We email or text only about business now. I have learned that seeing him leads to conversations that can buckle me for days. This week nothing has happened but my bud is out of town, and I'm in the apartment alone, and I haven't lived alone in fifteen years, and I'm not used to it, and I'm out walking around alone thinking about being alone, and when will I get used to it, and will I have to get used to it all over again after we have to give up the apartment, whenever that is, and am I just putting off the inevitable, but also honestly why do we all take so much pride in being fine alone, why can't we just say we're someone who doesn't like being alone, why can't we all *Golden Girls* it up before we're golden, why are we even on this earth if not to be with other people, and it's a lot of thinking, and this tends to lead to no good end, and now I'm crying on the street, again, and come back to find the kid waiting for me at the front gate and it turns out the kid has been crying on the street too, and we laugh about it and talk about being alone, the kid has never lived on her own before, and she does have a boyfriend who basically lives with her now, and she also has a lot of friends, and isn't alone all that much, but sometimes feels alone even if she's with other people, that thing, and I tell her what I've just been thinking about, why do we all think we have to be okay alone, and how much I like having the kid and her dad there, whether we're hanging out together or doing our own things separately in the same room, just knowing these people I love are there in the room makes me so happy, and why isn't that okay, and the kid says *It is okay*, and that she loves it too, the kid says sometimes she just gets sad and doesn't know why because everything is so good, and I tell her that's pretty normal, and remind the kid how much change she's been through in the last year or two, and how amazing she's actually doing, and the kid thanks me and says *I couldn't do it without you*, and I'm thinking she really could, but I'm really glad neither of us has to right now.

Kids Bring Laundry

The kid comes over to print out her valentine story for her boyfriend. *Ooh, your highlighter looks good,* she says. The kid has been teaching her about makeup.

Always tell me if it doesn't! she says.

You know I will. The kid asks for help putting together the valentine. Neither the kid nor the wife is a genius in the collating department. The kid has printed it out in what seems like the right way, two pages side by side like a book, but it doesn't work out when you fold it all together. *Oh shit,* she says.

No don't worry, we'll figure it out. It's like a math problem, the wife says. They start by putting numbers on each page, and it takes a minute to figure out that this project is nothing a glue stick won't fix. *Do you want to make a cover for it? I don't have my craft stuff here but I have this and that you could cut some hearts out of.* The wife has just made a batch of valentines for her girlfriends, her girlfriends have been so good to her this year, and you know, maybe she can be the change she wishes to see in her own world or some bullshit. The kid cuts out some hearts and flowers and fixes up the cover. She calls the next morning, because she's forgotten a paper for school, which the wife drops off on her way to get a mani-pedi because she's doing whatever the fuck she wants today.

———

The kid texts again later to ask if she and her boyfriend can come over and do laundry. The three of them hang out in the bed with the dog, making Instagram stories and talking about how cute rats are.

You have so many kids now, the boyfriend says.

I know, the wife says.

This is what parenting is, the kids bring over laundry.

I figured this out a few weeks back, she says.

We could have gone and dropped it off, the boyfriend adds. *We like hanging out with you guys.*

I know, she says. *I'm here for all of it.*

Coincidences

There are no coincidences. Her bud says this often. Not quite as often as the president says *no quid pro quo,* but often enough that perhaps the idea is the same, that if he says it often enough, she will believe it too. She knows their situation is sweet. She knows that the timing worked out nicely for her. Having company, having his specific company and the kid's specific company, is turning out to be vastly better than having only her own company. She is learning that she is a person who likes being in the company of others more than she likes not having the company of others. She works in solitude. She doesn't go to an office, doesn't have that kind of camaraderie (twice a year for ten days with her colleagues, major camaraderie, yes, the other 345 days of the year, no camaraderie), she liked her husband, she liked talking to him and not talking to him, she liked his particular presence. Her bud says, often, *The timing is too perfect to be a coincidence. You ended up in the city, in this apartment, right when I got to the city and needed a place to stay.* She points out that he can afford his own place, he points out that her point is a point toward his point. *You and me and my kid are all helping each other here. It's not about rent. This is about all of us. You're helping her so much. I'm so grateful to you.* Helping his kid is not a thing she has to try to do, it's a thing that just is. She loves the kid. You help people you love when they need you. Her bud helps her all the time. He listens good and holds her hand when she cries, which is still a daily occurrence, and he makes her laugh, and he watches rom-coms and award shows with her and he takes her to the movies and he makes her dinner and he buys her bagels and ice cream. Every day.

Secret

Near the end, when the husband and wife were still together and she was out of town, she didn't miss him in the way she once had. She was busy with work, she was with her friends, she would have liked it if he came with her more often but he didn't and eventually she let it go. It was never like, Oh I'm so happy to be away from that guy. She was always happy to see him when she got back. But it was harder being away from the dog.

Gesture

Rereading some of her parents' divorce documents, she's newly struck by the fact that she's again forgotten some critical points.

Is there a difference between blocking things out and just forgetting? People forget plenty of not-painful things.

Things forgotten: That her mom had taken a small handful of pills, said she didn't want to live, went to the hospital. Was diagnosed as a *gesture* rather than a genuine suicide attempt. (Note: It does line up that her mom would do this as a gesture. Imagine what you think an opera singer might be like at home, and then crank that up past ten. That said, there's little doubt that she never had a proper mental health diagnosis, or at least one that her daughter was ever made aware of, or at least one that resulted in her behaviors and moods changing overtly for the better.) Later told a neighbor she'd kill herself if she didn't get custody.

Things remembered: Letter from shrink indicating that her mom probably had postpartum depression at the very least, though neither of those words were used. That the shrink and her dad communicated about her mother without her knowledge. That her grandmother said her mother's efforts to avoid changing diapers were *adolescent,* and that her father corroborated that his daughter had ulcers and scars from those ulcers from repeatedly unchanged diapers. That her father has a list of dates her mother spent away from her from 1964 through 1967, which totaled approximately two and a half years when she was between the ages of three and six. That when she and her mom moved to New York, she wasn't allowed to see her dad until the divorce was final, meaning she didn't see him at all for most of 1968 and 1969. This part she actually remembers from life: She saw him once outside of her school, when he was in New York for a meeting with the lawyers. She was brought outside and talked to him through the fence and told him that her mom would be mad and he should probably go home. She wished she could go with him. But she didn't tell him that.

To review:

Mom gone for long stretches of time in early childhood, likely mental health issues.

Doesn't see Dad for long stretch of time in early elementary school.

Stays single until she's forty-one, hoping she'll know enough by then to get it right on the first try.

I Don't but I Do

I don't want to regret having married him but sometimes I do. I don't want to erase the last fifteen years, but I don't want to remember them now either. I don't want to remember things I thought were good and wonder if they weren't so good. I don't want to mention his name in casual conversation, but if I don't, then I have to heavily revise fifteen years' worth of stories, I have to make *we* into *I* and I think we all know how much I like *we*. I don't want to hate someone I loved but sometimes I do. I don't want to put my trust in someone new but I don't want to not trust someone new because one specific person broke my trust. I don't want to wonder if my marriage was good but now I do. I don't want to wonder if I was a terrible wife but now I do. I don't want to wonder who my husband is now but I do. I don't want to wonder if I never knew who my husband was, if he never knew me. I don't want to look at his Instagram photos, but sometimes I do. I don't want to construe stories about what photos of art or windows or inanimate objects mean in terms of our relationship, past, present, or future, but sometimes I do. I don't want to be married to someone who doesn't want to be married to me, but I don't want to get divorced. I don't want to be single, remember how single I once was? I don't want to go on fucking Tinder dates. Someone kill me before I do, because it will kill me and I don't want my obituary to say her husband left her and she was killed by Tinder, that she opened Tinder and swiped and swiped whichever way means no until she died. I know the great couple who met on Tinder. There are no more great Tinder couples. I don't want to date at all. I don't want to show someone my fifty-seven-year-old body and I don't want to get used to some new dude's weird body. I got used to one dude's weird body. Dudes' bodies are just weird. I don't want this to be a story about losing one dude and then meeting a new dude and then everything is better. I don't want this to be a story about losing a dude and then finding myself and then everything is better. I want a story without losing and without finding. I want this to be a story about everything just being better.

Less Wrong

She's been in the city for nine months now. It's always hard for her to see this city as forever. She's lost her faith in forever anyway. She's out of moves. She's here now, and it feels way less wrong than it has in the past. Less wrong is as close to right as she's got at this moment. It could be all the way right but let's not lose our minds here. She knows it's not forever, but reserves the right to return as needed.

Some Sort of Recovery

New York City, at times, most times, has been a place she has wanted to leave, but is now a place she has come to on purpose, for some sort of recovery. The loving attention from her bud does make her reconsider the kind of excitement that her husband wants. It is exciting when someone pays attention to you, a new person or a new old person or any person. It would be lovely, so lovely, if she could believe that any new person would be the thing that fixes everything. Nothing is fixed. Nothing was broken. Everything was good and then one big part of that got broken by one person on purpose. Well, we don't know if that's true. That's today's story. We may never know if that's true. We still don't know what's true. Maybe her marriage was broken. She didn't feel that she was broken, she felt closer to whole as she got older. There was a time in her life when she did believe that the relationship part of her was broken, in some invisible way that was not ever going to be repaired, and not for lack of trying. Then she met someone and stopped believing that. Look, she thought, I'm not broken after all! I'm doing this! I'm pretty good at it! Then that someone left. It was all a big fake-out. Now she's spending time with a new (old) person and it can be extremely pleasant to spend time with a new (old) person, and then the morning comes and things are not fixed, grief still exists. They are not sleeping together, though it's not like the idea of sleeping together isn't there. It is there. Or it's there in her mind. Or it's in your mind. It's in your mind, right? It's surely in your mind. Will-they-won't-they-when-will-they-already is part of the template. They are affectionate in a way she's never been in a platonic friendship before, but there's a boundary, even if it's a flexible boundary, and it's enjoyable. He's not her boyfriend. We can't call it a relationship but it's not not a relationship. All friendships are relationships. They sleep with whomever they want *except* for each other, and then they come home. Except no one is sleeping with anyone else. Or she's not. He might be. But he's always there. She doesn't want to think about what he does with anyone else. She wants him to want to have sex with her. (I mean, she wants everyone to want to have sex with her, in the same way that she wants to be invited to more parties and then not go.) She might want to have sex with him? Someday? He might or might not want to have sex with her, someday? She might want to have sex with no one ever again, on any day? He doesn't want a relationship with anyone right now, full stop. Sorry, were you thinking this was going to be the love part of the eating and praying, did you think she was going to get her groove back? She doesn't want any more endings unless they're happy. Is this because she never writes happy endings, be-cause she writes vague endings? Should she write herself a happy ending? Knowing full well that the rest of her story will write itself however it wants to? And that she'll probably write all that nonsense down and then that story will change and she'll have to rewrite the whole damn thing yet again? She doesn't want to regret having loved, but sometimes she does, she doesn't want to fear loving again but you know she does. She doesn't want to start her life over, but it's already too late for that.

This Story Has Changed, Again

Should we start over? Is that what this story wants to be about? Starting over? It feels too late to start over. Better it should just keep changing.

Only What Is

What if she had just kept cooking all these years? What if she'd come to love hiking and hadn't really tried? What if she'd just gotten some damn *Cosmo* magazine and learned ten ways to spice up your marriage, how to learn the art of seduction? What if she'd said *I think we're a little bit stalled*? What if she'd told her husband she wasn't super satisfied with their sex life lately instead of asking him if he was satisfied with their sex life? What if she'd allowed herself to sit for a beat with his every *It's fine*, spent time with *fine* as not being so very fine of an answer? What if she'd admitted that she was a little bit less happy in the marriage than she had once been too? What if somewhere in herself that she can't access, she doesn't want to be with him now, not because she's no longer wanted by him, but like, separate from what he wants, or maybe alongside it? What if she doesn't know what she wants now? What if she never does? What if he loved her more? What's the measure for that? Is that a bad thing? It doesn't feel like a good one. The first time she realized she loved him, they hadn't been dating long at all, maybe a week or two. It was one of those days when he'd just stopped by, and when she closed the door after he left, she thought, I *love* that guy! *Love* is italicized here but you should really try to hear it with an upward inflection, the way she heard herself say it in her head, like it was not necessarily romantic love but the way you'd say it about the bagel guy who remembers your name and sometimes puts a black-and-white cookie in with your order just because. It was only in the next moment that she thought, Oh, oh, maybe I am in love, because it's not like she had ever really been sure what that meant anyway, and maybe all we're trying to say now is that maybe being loved just felt so good that she thought she was in love the whole time but really wasn't. Arguably, this seems like a stretch. She doesn't doubt that she loved him. Maybe everyone wonders what love even is after it goes away. Maybe there's a period of time where heartbreak supersedes recognition of any other emotional component of an experience. When he left, she'd been so mired in hurt that it was harder to locate any other feeling in the thick of that mud. And in this brain, it's just so much easier to keep rolling steady in the hurt lane than it is to merge into accountability. So what if this had to happen, was always going to happen, what if there's no other way for this to have happened than for him to blow it up? What if her bud is right, what if this was all meant to be, what if god *was* involved? Who is she to say god isn't involved if god is involved? Wouldn't god be like *So rude, I'm out here hooking you up and everyone besides you is telling you it's god and you're all like "That's not god that's just random," and I'm like "Bitch, god is good, god is love, jeez, c'mon!"* One of her friends had said *Who knows if there's a god, who knows if everything happens for a reason, but isn't it more fun to think that there might be a good reason for things than to think that there might not be?* What if all the people who believed in something greater than themselves were right, what if all the ones who believed in nothing were wrong? What if everyone was right, that god isn't everything or nothing, it's everything *and* nothing? What if there were no what if, what if there were only what is?

What if is her game. What if is her fucking brand. What if is what stories are. What if she spoke up more, or louder, or longer or what if she did one little thing, one little something, one little anything differently and the words on this page are all *what if*s that mercifully never got thought because they stay together? But she didn't, and they don't.

All We Have to Do

All you have to do is just tell me you aren't happy before she comes into the picture. That's all you have to do. All you have to do, when you ask me what I think is wrong with you, and I say *I don't know, why don't you talk to your therapist*, is call your therapist. That's all you have to do. All I have to do is just tell you I think you might be depressed, before she comes into the picture, that I think maybe possibly maybe we might be in trouble, before she comes into the picture. That's all I have to do. All I have to do and all you have to do, all one of us has to do is just tell the other the truth. That's all we have to do. All we have to do is know the truth and admit to each other the truth. All we have to know and to admit is that something isn't right, even if some other things are right, even if we don't know what isn't right. All we have to know is that there is enough that's still more than right to start working on what isn't right. All we have to do is travel back in time and tell each other the truth and then work on what isn't right before she comes into the picture. Whatever happens from here we can say that we tried. And after that, all we have to do is let go.

Mexico

Her husband's name appears on her phone or email infrequently now, but a small panic always rises when it does. What now. This time, he wants to let her know he's taking a vacation to Mexico later this month, and that he'll put an amount equal to the cost of that trip in checking for her to use as she wants. Their finances are still combined. They contribute equally. He has been, overall, as reasonable as he's ever been about money, post-split. This doesn't mean she's not totally fearful of this changing at any moment. But this isn't really the point.

When they were in couples therapy, and it came up that they hadn't taken a real vacation together since their honeymoon, the fine therapist aka shitty therapist number one said something to the effect of *Okay, you really need to plan a vacation.* So they planned a vacation. Locations were considered and rejected. Mexico was chosen. Complications ensued. Dates didn't work. Hotels were rejected. Maine was chosen. Deposits were made. Deposits were returned. No trip was taken. *I'm going on vacation to Mexico* lands in her email box. A kick to the head lands in her teeth.

Every Little Thing

She's having a week. She's had a misleading period of not crying for several days in a row and then she gets the Mexico email that reminds her she's been rejected. They couldn't make it happen to go on a vacation for fifteen years but in just over six months apart her husband has booked a vacation for himself with someone else. Rejection is an aspect of this whole shitty deal that she doesn't like to spend a lot of time on because she can go from *I am an amazing and talented writer and sometimes even semi-decent human* to *Obviously, I am not worthy of romantic love.* Her fifteen-year marriage is the longest relationship of her life by fifteen years, unless you count one relationship that lasted a year and a half with four breakups. She has an old story going in her head about how she broke the first two hearts that ever came her way, two dear, lovely boys sent to her by god in high school and then college, and that having rejected god's gift of these dear, lovely boys, she would now endure a loveless lifetime of heartache and rejection. Subsequent to this, over the next twenty years of dating, she is broken up with countless times, she breaks up with only two more men, one of whom seems truly heartbroken but ends the breakup lunch consoling her. So much easier not to be the one who causes pain. Which leads her to wonder, yet again, what her husband tells himself about causing her this kind of pain, because he often says he's not causing it at all. He usually says he's sorry she's in pain. Her friends, across the board, blame him. She believes they believe this. She knows the marriage ended because he wanted it to end. She has many, many versions of *what his deal is* that exist in her head; some of them exonerate her from the blame. She has tried to be a good partner. But sometimes after all these years she still thinks some larger force doesn't want her to have this kind of love. It is a bubble bath, get under the covers early and watch TV in the dark kind of night.

Her bud and the kid and her boyfriend and the rapper bound through the door making noise. *We're home! Where are you? What are you doing in there? It's only ten o'clock! Everyone, into the bed!* Everyone piles into the bed. Three teenagers and her old bud. *What are you doing in here in the dark?*

I'm just in a mood.

Don't worry . . . one of them sings.

About a thing, everyone joins in. *'Cause every little thing, is gonna be alright.*

This is totally ruining her blue-mood plans, this party in her bed. It's more than ruining them. Every little thing is alright, right now.

The kids are going to a young people's sober convention this weekend. The rapper drops his rap for the sober rap battle. (*Ya sponsor just called me, told me he got ninety days, asked me how to hide his relapse, I told him ninety ways.*) Everyone cheers. The party breaks up and the kids go into the bathroom to do who knows what, they're being sort of quietly giggly, the kid emerges laughing with her hair done like Trump at one point, goes back in, they softly sing Leonard Cohen's "Hallelujah," in harmony.

Twenty-Seven

Her bud says they have to celebrate her sober anniversary. She says *Ah, we can just go to our meeting tomorrow*, he does this pretend-angry thing that he does, insists they have to celebrate, gets movie tickets, takes her to one of her favorite neighborhood places. They have favorite neighborhood places. She always wondered why she and her husband could never find favorite neighborhood places when they lived there. It's the East Village. They had places, just not ones they were excited to call their places. They found some when they moved to Brooklyn. But her bud is a solid finder of places.

Happy anniversary. That's amazing.

Thanks. I feel like I'm actually only twenty-seven years old.

I'm sorry you almost drank over me.

Ahahahahahaha yeah no that didn't happen.

Oh right you liked our other friend better.

Listen, if I didn't drink over my husband, I'm probably not going to drink over any guy.

Oh yeah, that guy. For a moment I forgot he existed. Now it's like a horrible song I can't get out of my head.

Okay well let's both go back to trying to forget.

Northern Sky

The wife and her bud settle in to watch a rom-com he likes that she hasn't seen. He has one favorite he's seen fifty times, several others on a second tier below that favorite. It's a sweet thing, the rom-com thing; he loves them, watches them for comfort. The wife watches *The Walking Dead* for comfort. She likes a great rom-com too, but romance is not her idea of comfort right now. They're sweet and hopeful and sometimes corny AF and sometimes perpetuate extremely unrealistic ideas about love. She wants to be sweet and hopeful and she knows she's sometimes corny but right now her ideas about love are messed up to say the least. This particular rom-com is about a couple trying to figure out by fate if they're meant to be together by fate. That sentence has actually been edited. You read it correctly. It's set in New York City, as they often are. There's Wollman Rink, where she fell on the ice when she was in sixth grade, there's Serendipity, where she had her first date ever, there are all her favorite bookstores that don't exist anymore. It's a sweet enough movie, and at the end when the couple comes together, clearly by fate, a Nick Drake song plays that her dear punk friends sang at their wedding. Her bud is holding her hand. She chokes out an explanation of why she's crying, he squeezes her hand harder. She hasn't cried for a couple days, since the kids came around singing. She doesn't want her bud to feel like his rom-com comfort plan failed. She doesn't want to wonder if it means anything that this song was in this movie about romantic fate, or that she's sitting there listening to it holding hands with someone who isn't her husband.

Rockefeller

You have used the word *love* in many different ways in many different contexts to mean many different things, but when your husband leaves after fifteen years, you maybe aren't so sure you know much about it anymore. You do know a lot of people use that word in your direction, a lot of them. A lot of them. And sure. Your friends love you. It's genuine, you know this, they love you, you love them. But there are levels, and this year, with the husband leaving, the levels of love received feel disproportionate to whatever levels of love you might have ever given out, lifetime. It knocks you over and down, the love, it's too much, and you are obviously an impostor. You have the unique gift, you are sure, of knowing how to *seem* real, to *seem* loving and warm and friendly, but it raises concerns, if your primary purpose is to be thought of as a decent human, versus actually being a decent human. You have had an idea of yourself as bright enough and sort of fun to be around, but could you have been that good a friend to that many people, or did you somehow con a whole lot of people? One friend says *Well if you did, either we're all a bunch of dopes or you're an evil genius.* But your friends are not dopes and you are not a genius of any kind, unless *evil genius* is actually so accurate that even you don't know it, like you're a host body for evil, and it comes in the form of faking people out so you can get invited to beach houses and lake houses and Italian villas.

Maybe you're like that guy who pretended to be a Rockefeller, except not on purpose. You know you're really just averagely kind, an average friend, averagely everything. You could even be okay with that, maybe we could all just try to level up to averagely kind, but having absorbed a lifetime of messages that say that we really shouldn't be okay with averagely anything, that we should be happy and perfect and for sure we should be lily white and we should probably not be women if possible, you get to a place where the wrongness of you feels like the most real thing, and then when people love on you it's all too much and you're baffled and feel undeserving and then what the fuck.

I Miss You

It was inevitable. It's my own fucking fault. I tell him I'm struggling, he tells me he misses me. I don't want to hear it, I deeply want to hear it. Where to put it, though. Safe-deposit box? Lingerie drawer? With the utensils?

A Walk in the Park

She says *I thought we were going to grow old together, take care of each other.*

The husband says *We still could.* Why doesn't she ask what that means? He says *I think some of the things I was asking of you were things I should have been looking at in myself.* He says it's harder being alone than he thought. He says he's having trouble really connecting with friends. He says it really *was* good between them. He says he wishes he'd suggested they cook together instead of asking her to do it. He seems like he's going to cry and then he doesn't. He says he's not against reconciliation some-day but doesn't know what that would look like.

She says *I have some ideas.*

Bits of Dialogue from a Car Ride that Shouldn't Have Happened a Year after He Moved Out Because She Let Herself Get False Hope after He Recently Acknowledged that He'd Projected Some of His Stuff onto Her

I don't understand!

My friends all understand.

Can you get one of them to explain it to me then?

I woke up one day and didn't want to be married anymore. That's it.

If I hurt you, truly, I want to know how, so I don't make the same mistakes with someone else.

You can think I'm an asshole if you want. Maybe you should.

I don't. Want to.

You can make up any stories about me that you want.

I don't want to make up stories about my marriage. I want the true story this time.

Maybe the Dog

Here is a story about the wife: sometimes when you hurt her, she has the ability to show patience and compassion, to try not to take it personally, to forgive. For sure, key words: ability, try, sometimes.

When you hurt someone she loves, that's another story altogether. In that story, she has the ability to show anger, righteousness. In that story, she will defend the person she loves. In that story, maybe only through that story, will she come to see that she must defend herself as well. That what is not okay for her loved ones is also not okay for her.

In this story, the someone she loves is the dog.

No dogs have been harmed in the making of this story. We need you to know this. The dog has been in the good care of the wife since the split. The harm done to the dog is at the level of indifference. The harm done to the dog is only that the husband now says he no longer feels strongly about the dog, feels the dog is a burden, likes the dog about as much as any other dog, would just as soon not dog-sit again in the future, but will honor his obligation, up to you. There's no harm done at all, not really. So maybe we should say it like this: the dog doesn't know he's been harmed. Or maybe he does. Maybe the dog understands things about harms done that we can never know. Maybe the dog has the answers she's been looking for all this time, and just can't put it into words. Maybe this is what had to happen for the wife to get it.

Arguments

Lifetime, she has not had many. There were enough between her mom and stepdad growing up for her to arrange a lifetime of avoiding them. This is in no way meant to imply that she has lived a life free of conflict. It is meant to indicate that as necessary, she was prepared to wait for a partner of her exact type and kind, or to move to another city to avoid dealing with it.

Notable arguments include:

1. Screaming at mom and stepdad in front of a sushi restaurant on Broadway about her not having health insurance (they were right, ish)
2. Screaming at a close girlfriend in front of a boutique on Columbus and 72nd Street (reason not remembered)
3. Screaming at a long-ago boyfriend in front of her building on Oakley and Erie in Chicago (reason not remembered)
4. Screaming at husband, in the second shitty therapist's office, and almost screaming at the shitty therapist as well (reason having something to do with money)

There is an argument with her bud. It begins with a news story and ends with insults. Her bud says she lives in fantasy. *You're being like Kellyanne*

Conway, he says. *You're a fucking asshole,* she says. She has never in her life said these words out loud to another human. She hears them as they come out of her mouth, quickly losing traction and volume on the way; her brain is on a delay, knows only as the words are on their way out that they should not be said. The regret happens while the words are being said. She takes the dog to the park and calls a friend. *He's obviously going to have to move out,* she tells the friend, who talks her through it, makes her laugh, and tells her to go home and make amends. *Everything will be fine. You've been friends for thirty years.* It's a good hour before she returns to the apartment, but by then she is eager to apologize. Unfortunately, her bud has also gone out, so she's about to text him when she finds an apologetic Post-it note on the counter with a heart and a smiley face and *I know you didn't mean what you said* and *I love you.* They hug when he comes home and she tells him she never fights with anyone and he laughs and tells her that wasn't a fight, that was just a lively dinner conversation at his family's house growing up. She wonders now if a few more lively conversations with her husband might have helped.

Revision

I don't think you'd be a good mother has been in my head for years now, long past my husband's numerous amends, which I accepted and appreciated. I always knew he was genuinely remorseful about it.

The thing is, he never said it. I know this now. He never said it. I learned, just now, via my journal, that this conversation, the original conversation where this good-mother topic came up, just a few months into our relationship, was not how I remembered it.

How it actually went: We were in his bed. We were talking about porn (whether to watch, what to watch if we did watch, what we might like to do after or during if we did watch), and about moving to a small town someday (where to move, when someday might be, what that would be like).

What will we do there? I said. Pretty sure neither of us imagined then that *get divorced* was what we would end up doing there. We were still imagining our happy ending.

You can watch the kids while I build stuff. Long pause while I considered what this meant, and he considered what he was going to say next. *Well, I'm not sure if I see us having kids.* He had, up to this point, talked often about us having kids.

Don't you think I'd be a good mom? I said.

I do, but I think you'd worry a lot, he said.

Fair enough. I worry excessively about many things. Now including the kid, who isn't even my own.

Review: *I don't think you'd be a good mother.* Said by no one. Construed, it seems, from some combination of my own thoughts and his use of *worry.*

I feel like I should apologize. Not to him, I mean, I should do that too, but I feel like I should apologize for getting this far and putting the car in reverse. Maybe just to myself. I'm not a fan of egregious twists, especially when it means I have to review a few decades of my life. I put something on someone else, on my partner, I held on to this idea I thought my partner believed about me, when it was actually what I believed about me. I had always been deeply unsure about my potential as a parent. The decision not to have children was one we made together, though it may have been a decision that got put off too long to know whether it was a real decision or a nondecision. My memory goes straight from *Okay, we'll put this off until after we do a few more things* to *I'm not sorry we never had kids.* But those last words were his, not mine. I'm not sorry we didn't put kids through divorce. I have, to an extent, defined myself by having been that kid. I have a measure of acceptance that we didn't have kids. I worry a lot, but I don't worry that I fucked up my kids. I have a larger measure of regret that I let the conversation fade out the way it did, that I didn't try to circle back around at some point. Prior to getting married, I had considered, and ultimately rejected, the idea of being a single mom as being more of a challenge than I was up for, and, by extension, knew I was most likely letting go of the idea of being a mom at all. I was in my late thirties then, and I knew if I found a partner that I wanted to have time with that person before we had kids. And I am glad, so glad I had time with that person before we forgot to keep talking about it. Regret is a funny thing. My program promises me that if we stay sober, we'll neither regret the past nor wish to shut the door on it. I well know that sharing my experiences can have value for another alcoholic who wonders if they too can get through a similar experience sober. But I for sure wish to shut the door on it sometimes. I wish to slam the door on it sometimes. One of the things about being sober is, those feelings we drank away, we start feeling them. It's not easy to be fully conscious twenty-four seven. Maybe I did slam the door on this subject in a certain way. Acceptance, the other side of regret, for me comes and goes. For every choice made, who knows how many more are let go that might have opened that door to something better. I don't know how not to wonder about other choices, or how not to wish now that I'd talked to my partner about this and so many other things when I had the chance, or how not to wish that I had talked to my therapist about how much time I spent wondering whether I should have kids, and whether or not I'd be a good mom, since the answer I usually arrived at was never that I'd be a great mom, it was that I'd probably be just as complicated a parent-person as my mom was. And as much as I know my mom did the best she could, don't we all want to do at least a little better than *best we could*? *Best we could* always feels both loving and sad at the same time. Seemingly, there was only one way to find out if I'd be a good mom, but I failed to definitively choose motherhood, and then I failed to fully make peace with that choice. That's regret, right? And yet, I couldn't get up in the morning if I didn't have some acceptance about my choices, or if those choices hadn't also led to so many joys and delights and wonders. And then a kid did come into my life, and she told me a new story about me.

I'm Telling You

She and the kid are out shopping again; the kid needs some socks. The kid says *thank you* often, and *I'm sorry* way more than anyone ever should. Everyone in her life tries to help her understand the difference between when to apologize and when there's not one thing to apologize for. Today she's thanking the wife for going shopping with her.

You mean so much to me. So much. You're like a sister and an aunt and a mom all together.

She tells the kid she loves her, again, that she'd do anything she could for her.

You know, I thought it was my husband who didn't think I'd be a good mom. But it was me. It was me. It was never him. I read it in my journal.

The kid grabs her by both arms, stops her in the middle of the store.

I'm telling you right now. I'm telling you. You're an amazing mom.

Season Finale

The kid has her own apartment, is probably starring in a spin-off as well, but as you now know, she's a major crossover character in this one. Kid's dad and soon-to-be divorcée are legit roommates now, kid's dad tells soon-to-be divorcée many times, over the course of the first season, that this is all happening for a reason, that everything happens for a reason. This is meant genuinely, and with no intent to discount free will, but rather to convey that at least in this particular situation, many positive things have resulted. Yet here please let us refer you to almost all the books she's ever written for the recurring theme of *NO IT DOES NOT.* In the second episode, the soon-to-be divorcée maybe rolls her eyes toward the camera, she's choosing her battles now due to the overarching battle of being soonly divorced, in the third episode she says something patronizing like *It's sweet that you think that,* and in the fourth episode she's like *OKAY THEN THE PRESIDENT WHAT IS THE REASON THE PRESIDENT IS HAPPENING,* meaning this to stand in for any and all terrible things that happen for no good reason. But by the end of the first season, having established and explored the god-no-god issue that heightens the will-they-won't-they, and for maybe the first time ever in her life, she has softened on the idea by some small degree, at least enough to acknowledge that a beautiful thing has transpired post–shitty thing, regardless of any evidence connecting those events and regardless of her position on this adage, she knows she is receiving something special, something she couldn't have known she needed in the wake of this massively shitty life change. Her old bud and his kid have turned up in the apartment and they have become a family of sorts, a family where the individual members, only some of whom are related by blood, decide separately and together what a family is, and it's such a particular kind of gift that if you'd asked her a year ago *Okay, if we take away your husband but you get to have this new weird little family experience with these people, you have to trust us that it's a gift, one whose meaning will become clear over time, what would you do*, she'd have been like *Yeah, I think I'll keep my husband*, but then she wouldn't have known about this gift, or what it would ultimately mean for her life, which she still doesn't, not really, but anyway not to spoil anything but by the time spring rolls around, if you came back and asked her then *Okay, now, if we took away your weird little family gift and gave you back your husband and your exact same life*, she'd say that was beyond her imagination.

This Story Will End

This story wants so much to have a happy ending but it's probably just going to have an ending. Maybe the happy part comes at the beginning of the next one.

Options

Once upon a time you were one half of a pretty happy couple who stayed together for fifteen years and then your husband went through a thing and decided to leave, but it didn't go exactly how he thought it would go, or maybe he didn't know exactly how it would go, or at least you knew it might not go how he thought it would go, that's probably closer to it, and after a year he was less sure about what he wanted or at least couldn't explain what he wanted, which made you more sure that he never knew what he wanted, but by this point, you weren't so sure what you wanted either anymore. You had wanted to try working it out from the beginning, but your husband was never fully willing to try. So you spent the year grieving and trying to stay in your life, painful as it was, and he spent the year doing you're not sure what with you're not sure whom, but occasionally expressing that he missed having you in his life. You and your husband would try to have conversations and sometimes they'd feel productive and sometimes they would feel the opposite of productive and so at those times when they felt productive, like you were as close to making peace with him as you could, you'd try to stick, like you had a halfway decent poker hand, and try to remind yourself the next conversation might not go as well. And then you came to an opening, one where it seemed like there might be the tiniest chance for reconciliation, even though he didn't say it, he didn't not say it.

You imagine yourself in the office of couples therapist number three, who asks you both what your goals are. Your husband says he wants you in his life, that's all he knows. You say you want him in your life too, but there's still one point on which you can't budge: monogamy. The third couples therapist, who because they are currently imaginary, is blessedly not shitty, asks the husband if he can be open to that, if he would be willing to discuss finding ways to reconfigure the relationship that would satisfy you both, within that confine. Your husband hesitates but says he would at least be willing to discuss that, if you are willing to explore any and all options for building something entirely new. You say *I think so? Are you?* He says *I think so?* You both giggle like you used to. There hasn't been a lot of giggling together over the last year, which is to say there's been no giggling. Giggling seems hopeful. You are profoundly fearful that the trust you once had can never be rebuilt, not with him, not with anyone. You are profoundly fearful that you'll never find your way back to each other now, you are profoundly fearful of a life without him, you are profoundly fearful . . . you are profoundly fearful. You once drove across the country with a dude you barely knew, in a car with a broken rearview mirror that cost him fifty bucks. Are you not going to try one more time with your husband of fifteen years, if he's open to it?

If you can't wait a minute longer to make a decision, then just make a fucking decision.

If you decide to trust that god has you covered, turn to page not-likely hundred.

If there's no question that you'd try again with your husband if you're actually still open to it after X time has passed, if he's actually still open to it after reading this, turn to some distant and imaginary future where you both have no questions about anything.

If you need to know how it turns out right now, please wait for one of you to die.

On the Eve of the Shitty Anniversary

The housebud is away.

A friend arrives from Kalamazoo.

The kids arrive from across town, bearing laundry, again. The wife and the kids catch up on some developments. There are always developments. The kids eat snacks, leave for a meeting. The kids return with more kids. The kids leave again because now there are no snacks. Three of the kids return to finish the laundry. It is now well past midnight. Kalamazoo friend and the wife are in the big bed catching up. The remaining kids come in and perform T-Pain's "Buy U a Drank," in its entirety, with choreography, before they leave.

She has been wondering what her life is going to be, post-marriage. Her husband moved out a year ago. She's been living in NYC with her bud for most of that year, house mom for most of that year. She still doesn't know where she'll be sleeping at the end of the year. She'll be sleeping in the apartment or she won't. She'll be sleeping in her own house or she won't. She thought she was going to be sleeping next to the same person forever and she isn't. This is what her life is right now.

It Says Love.

I get another new tattoo, my second post-split, spur of the moment. My dad's handwriting, actual size, from one of his letters to me when I was a kid. It says *love.* With a period after it, like a decree. I still believe in it. Sometimes like Santa. But I do.

Again

The time is coming to give up the apartment. There has long been some denial about this. *No. We are going to live here forever,* her bud has said, more than a few times. But the wife has already begun spending more time upstate where it's easier to care for the dog, whose mobility is more limited now; there's a ramp off the back porch, so he can more easily go outside.

We're going to have to be friends who make plans now, she tells her bud. It isn't that they don't already make some plans ahead of time, but their favorite plan is no plan, just hanging out at the end of the day watching a movie, ordering in. Plans are made with the kid, but her dad is away both times she's back in the city. We have just been told not to touch things, especially our faces. She and the kid have dinner. They hug. They don't know that it's the last time for a while.

She Could See the Sky

The soon-to-be exes decide to co-own the house, but only the wife will live there, until she doesn't. Maybe someday there will be more details, more understanding, of how the husband and the wife arrived at this. The short version: over a period of months, there are a number of long, emotionally grueling conversations that should probably have happened years ago, or in couples therapy, or something. No hard-and-fast conclusions are drawn in these conversations. The hardest and fastest conclusion is that on balance, perhaps these two were reasonable enough, had had enough love, had accumulated a few tools to help them get to a place where they were able to say some hard things, and hear some hard things, and emerge without animosity. Mostly. Without more animosity than one might expect a few years later when you hope you'll be mostly over it.

The husband had renovated most of the kitchen while they were together. Some upper-level cabinets and the windows he planned to build remained unbuilt. Over time, the husband built the windows and installed the windows, and these windows were the real deal, built-from-scratch windows, and they were not just way better than the crap replacement windows that had been put in long before they moved in, they were bigger, made to fit the original window opening that had been bricked up around the smaller, crap replacement windows. And what happened when she went home and looked out the windows almost made her feel like there had never been any windows in there at all. She could see the sky.

Acknowledgments

Where to begin to offer measly thanks to the ridiculous numbers of people who helped me with this book and/or through this crap time in my life. This book would not exist without the boatloads of love and support that came my way; turns out writing nonfiction about an emotionally painful period of your life is—wait for it—emotionally painful.

Nina Solomon, thank you for the countless reads and rereads, and for being the amazing, genuine cheerleader that you are, and for mumble mumble decades of friendship. I just could not have gotten through any part of this without you. Cannot. Will not. Ever. You are my favorite for ever and for true, till Lois Lane.

Readers: Megan Stielstra, role model. David Ulin, your thoughtful notes were invaluable. Lindsay Muscato, Anne Hensley, Gina Frangello, Emily Rapp Black, Allison Mackie, your eyes and thoughts and support helped me more than you can possibly imagine.

Bob Leonard and Gaby Salick—you have no idea what you did for me. No idea. Your generosity is off the charts. I wrote a book in your apartment that probably wouldn't exist otherwise.

Gift-givers, card-senders, food-bringers, people who called and FaceTimed and texted and emailed kind thoughts: There were so so so many and hopefully I remembered to send proper notes for the gifts, but for the rest: know that every single good thought that was sent to me during this crap time meant so much to me, every last Facebook comment and DM.

Ted Bonar and Lea Dooley—I mean. You don't know. But I still dream of that lake and your good care, and Percy is probably still dreaming of it too, wherever he is now. Jen Pastiloff and all the beautiful women of the Tuscany trip, hard agree on life-changing. Chanda Prescod-Weinstein, Sarah Thyre, Jenn-Anne Gledhill, and Liz Cochran, your daily texts and thoughts and phone calls carried me. Rebecca Brown, your kindness is unmatched. Tod Goldberg and the rest of my dear UCR colleagues, Jill Essbaum, the KarZaps, Mary Otis, Joshua Malkin. Ken Foster, Julia Lane, Sarah Jaffe, Nelly Reifler, Amanda Stern, Lisa Lucas, Roy Kesey, Maret Orliss, Kiese Laymon, Rick Moody, Jade Chang, Nina Revoyr, Felicia Luna Lemus, Rachel Kann, Susan Kiyo Ito. Henslies, Emily Kastner, Casey Claussen, and all my Kalamazoo frens, each of you extended needed wisdoms and kindnesses. Caroline Leavitt: bringer of literary generosity and cardigans. Michele Filgate, Wendy Ortiz, Cari Luna, Bernadette Murphy, Donny Ward!, Joe Danisi, Jeanne Tripplehorn, Jon Ross, Victoria Loustalot!, Emily Rapp Black and Anne Hensley, double thanks to each of you for soup and books and linens and more. Luke, thank you for letting me include your hilarious words. Erin Williams, Melissa Febos, Leslie Jamison, Mary Karr, you don't even know how much you helped me late in the game. Catherine Texier, and your lovely audience that magical night, you gave me the confidence to put this out there. Beloved former students, now friends: Heather Scott Partington, who never doesn't send a card; Charli Engelhorn and Annemarie Hauser, I will never ever forget your kindness at that graduation, never; Sarah Sheppeck, for love and breakfasts.

Many thanks to David L. Ulin and *air/light* for publishing the excerpt.

Stephen Mailer: for rides all over the tristate area, some of them poopy. Michael Connors, Jenny Bransford, Michael Knight, Michelle

Esrick, Lusia Strus, Karin Riggs, Suzanne Setterstrom, Lizzie Maya, Thomas Dunning, Shayne Adams, Nora O'Connor, Alex Beechko, Krissy Shields, Hal Strickland, Lonnie McDonald, your love and light. Frank Vitolo, forget about it. My East Village friends, my Upper West Side friends, my beloved Apocalypse friends, my Chicago friends, all my new nighttime friends, you have all listened and seen me and loved me with your huge, open hearts, and my gratitude is boundless.

Sarita Bhakuni: your support and generosity are beyond measure.

Alice Tasman, you are the best of the best and I adore you always; thank you for a couple decades of doing what you do so well. Remember lunches?

Dan Smetanka, this book would just not be what it is without your brilliant, thoughtful guidance. Leigh Newman, Andy Hunter, Laura Berry, Olivia Rollins, Dan López, Wah-Ming Chang, Rachel Fershleiser, Megan Fishmann, Selihah White, and the entire awesome Counterpoint team, my great appreciation is ongoing!

My buddy Percy: RIP, sweet boy. Thank you for sticking around just long enough. Pearl, thank you for overseeing my edits and keeping me warm in a pandemic. (Yes. These are my dogs.)

Ben, I'm not sure how many exes would be as cool as you have been about this, so I remain grateful for that, and for many, many beautiful years.

To my family, thank you for loving me. I love you back.

Michael and Janie Hurley, no amount of gushing could fully convey my love and gratitude. The love and joy you brought into my life in that sad year is unquantifiable. Gracie, I love you too, and in my world the sister of my pretend kid is also my pretend kid.

© Allison Mackie

ELIZABETH CRANE is the author of six works of fiction, most recently the novel *The History of Great Things* and the story collection *Turf*. She is a recipient of the Chicago Public Library Foundation 21st Century Award. Her work has been featured on NPR's *Selected Shorts* and adapted for the stage by Chicago's Steppenwolf Theatre. Her novel, *We Only Know So Much*, has been adapted for film. She teaches in the low-residency master's program at UC Riverside–Palm Desert. She lives in Upstate New York with her dog, Pearl. Find out more at elizabethcrane.com.